M3 MACBOOK AIR FOR BEGINNERS AND SENIORS

Detailed Guide with Comprehensive Illustrations on How to Setup and Use your device (macOS 14 Sonoma Manual) With Tips and Tricks for MacBook Air users

SCOTT WHETZEL

Table of Contents

Introduction 1

MacBook Air (13- & 15-inch) Specifications 2

Additional features and what to expect 2

Chapter 1 5

Upgrading to the new macOS Sonoma 5

Check out which device is Compatible with the new macOS 14 5

Check if macOs Sonoma can work on your Mac 5

Downloading & installing the new macOS Sonoma.6

Installing Mac OS X Sonoma 7

Set up macOS 14 8

Your macOS software Update to the newest version 9

Using software updates 9

Should the Software Update not appear 10

Chapter 2 11

Turn on or off your MacBook gadget 11

Toggle on your device 11

Toggle your Macbook off 12

Restarting your device after installation or upgrade 12

Charging your Macbook battery 13

Charge the battery 13

Exhibit the battery percentage via the menu bar. 13

Adjust the battery settings. 14

Optimize or Enhance Battery Charging 14

Low Power Mode 14

High Power Mode 14

View the battery-charged level 15

Battery life history...15

Reduce battery consumption.............................16

Chapter 3..18

Setup your new Macbook Air 18

Set or configure your Macbook Air for first-time
Mac users...18

Chapter 4..28

Knowing simple Gestures 28

Simple trackpad gestures on your new Macbook
gadget 28

CHAPTER 5...30

Managing and setting up Apple ID on a Mac 30

Creating or generating an Apple ID on your
Macbook Air 31

Configure your Apple ID's data on a Mac 32

Set up your Mac's Apple ID sign-in and security
details 33

Set up your Apple ID mailing address and payment
method on Mac 33

Organize your Apple ID's media and buying
preferences on a Mac 34

Log in or out of your Apple ID on a Mac 34

Login with your Apple ID 34

Signing out or Exiting your Apple ID 35

CHAPTER 6 36

APPLE PAY 36

Use Apple Pay on Your Mac and Set It Up 36

How to Configure Apple Pay in Mac Safari 36

Configure Touch ID with Apple Pay on a MacBook
....37

Enable Apple Pay on an earlier Mac 39

Enable iPhone-Based Apple Pay Payments on a Mac
....39

Enable Macbook Air Apple Watch Apple Pay
Payments 40

How to Use Your Mac to Manage Apple Pay Cards 41

Modify the Default Apple Pay Card on the Macbook
Air 42

Remove or Take a Card Out of your Mac Apple Pay
....43

Modify Your Shipping and Contact Detail 44

Adjusting or Modifying Your Billing Address 45

CHAPTER 6 47

iCloud 47

Storing folders in iCloud Drive on Mac 48

Configure iCloud Drive 48

Keep your Documents and Desktop folders on
iCloud Drive 48

Collaborate & share folders using iCloud 49

Allow individuals to work together in folders.....49

Accept a file or folder-sharing invitation 50

See and control the files you've shared..............50

Quit sharing a folder 51

View and manage the storage on your iCloud 51

Utilize Mac iCloud Photos 52

Activate iCloud Pictures. 52

Stop utilizing iCloud Pictures on your Mac 53

Stop using iCloud Pictures on all Apple laptops and gadgets..53

Chapter 7 54

Pairing or Link your Macbook Air computer to the internet 54

Utilize WiFi 54

Pair to an available WiFi network.......................54

Connect to a secret WiFi network 54

Utilize Ethernet to pair your Mac to the web......55

Utilize the Instant Hotspot...............................56

Chapter 8 61

Macbook Air Touch ID & trackpad 61

Make use of the Mac's trackpad and mouse motions 61

Trackpad gestures 61

Mouse gestures 62

Utilize Mac Touch ID..63

Configure Touch ID. 63

Change the name or remove fingerprints 65

Utilize Touch ID to open your Macbook, login, or swap users 65

Utilize Touch ID to generate procurement 66

CHAPTER 9 67

Stage Manager on Mac 67

How to Use Mac's Stage Manager 67

What is a Stage Manager? 67

How to Activate and Deactivate Stage Manager 67

How to Utilize a Single App with Stage Manager ... 71

How to Use Several Apps and Groups in Stage Manager 73

Using Stage Manager with several applications: 73

How to modify Mac Stage Manager Settings 76

CHAPTER 10 80

How to move data from your Old to your recently purchased Macbook Air 80

Moving or transferring files from one Macbook to a different one 80

Utilize Migration Assist. 81

Via Time Machine backup 81

How to Activate AirDrop 84

Sending a Folder via AirDrop 86

How to Disable Mac AirDrop 87

Making Use of Control Centre 87

How to Use the Finder 89

How to Move a File From a Mac Computer to an iPhone...91

Share or move folders via iPhone to your MacBook Air utilizing AirDrop..............................91

How to Move Files from iPhone to Mac Using Email 92

How to Sync Data Between an iPhone and a Mac..93

Use iCloud Photos to Transfer Images from iPhone to Mac...95

Move Files from iPhone to Mac Using iCloud Drive 97

Chapter 11 100

Setup Messages for Mac...100

Setup iMessage 100

Stop using iMessage..100

Message someone on a Mac...................................100

Texting or sending text to groups 101

Use Business Chat to send a text to a company ...102

Un-send or modify a message on Mac..................103

Undoing a sent text or SMS.............................103

Adjust a sent text or SMS 103

Utilize Tap-back in a text via your Macbook........103

Sending an audio message via your Macbook......105

Personalize the messages 105

Make your Memoji on Mac Messages...................106

Blocking text in messages on your Macbook........106

Control unwanted calls 107

Creating & controlling contacts in Mac Messages 107

Creating a fresh contact 107

Modify a person's name to look differently in the
sidebar 108

Chapter 12...109

Customize your display 109

Your Mac's System Preferences 109

Lock the screen...110

Select a screen protector 110

Remember your forgotten passwords 110

Sharing passphrase & passkeys with others.......111

Personalize the menu bar and Control Centre. .112

Update macOS...112

Family Sharing and iCloud configurations........112

Utilizing System Setups to personalize your
Macbook...113

Open System Preference on your Macbook to
locate options. 113

Locate a setting option in the System Settings..114

Select a recommended setting 115

Return to the Mac system settings that you previously
viewed...116

Navigate through the settings you were most
recently in 116

Select a setting from a list of previously seen
options 116

Adjust your system screen display language.........118

Choosing your preferred language for every application 118

Make your screen text & other icons bigger 119

Increasing display size & icons 119

Enlarge text and icons in all applications and system components 120

Enlarge text for certain applications or system components...120

Change the resolution of your Mac display 122

Adjust the resolution on your main monitor. ...122

Adjust the linked display's resolution. 122

CHAPTER 12..124

Split Screen 124

Utilize your Mac Split Screen................................124

Utilize Mission Control to Utilize Split-Screen on your gadget 126

Utilize Mission Control to split-screen via your new gadget: 126

How to Use a Mac in Split Screen Mode................127

CHAPTER 13..129

Taking a Screenshot on your Macbook Air 129

Taking a Mac Screenshot via Complete Screen 129

Custom Area Screenshot..130

Screenshot via menu bar pop-up............................130

How to Modify the Mac's Screenshot Save Location 131

Crop a Mac Screenshot 131

Making Use of the Integrated Screenshot Cropping Tool 131

Utilize Photos application to crop 133

CHAPTER 14 134

Personalize your Mac's wallpaper image 134

Mac wallpaper settings 135

Include a picture 135

Add an album or folder 136

Dynamic or Lively Wallpapers 136

Select a photo to utilize as your gadget's wallpaper. 136

Rotate Aerials 137

Photos 137

Colors 138

Pictures, Records, and Folders 138

Choose between a bright and dark theme for your Macbook 138

Modify Mac Night Shift settings 138

Setting up the Night Shift 139

Schedule 139

Turn on warmer hues on your Mac at a certain hour of the night 139

Switch to warmer colors on your Mac around sunset. 140

Adjust the color (hue) of your Macbook manually to warmer hues 141

Color (hue) temperature 141

CHAPTER 15..142

Widget...142

Adding and customizing widgets for Mac............142

Add or include widgets to your display desktop...143

Adding Notification Centre widgets....................143

Utilize Mac widgets for iPhones.........................144

Personalize widgets.......................................144

Take the Notification Center's widgets down....144

Modify the widget's settings. 144

Utilize a Mac screen saver...............................145

Personalize the Mac's screen saver...................145

CHAPTER 16..147

MUSIC...147

Find songs..147

Search Apple songs.......................................147

Check for songs via the iTunes.........................147

Select music from your preferred genres. 148

Find tracks in Music on Mac by using the column
browser...148

Discover music in Mac Music via the filters.........149

Use Mac Music to play music from your collection.
....149

Streaming suggested music from Apple Music.150

Play the Apple Music radio in Mac Music............151

Playing a station 151

Set up a station..151

Play music together on a Mac with SharePlay 151

Create SharePlay to launch automatically 152

Use Mac Music to listen to an online broadcast153

Change the volume of the Music........................153

Personalize your listening experience...................154

Shuffle or replay tracks via your music 154

Put your music in order in Music on Mac............155

Utilize the queue 155

Utilize Autoplay..155

Organize and add songs to the queue 155

View the music you've played lately....................156

Arrange tracks in Mac Music. 156

Sort using the pop-up menu 157

Sorting via clicking the column headers............157

Find the Music files...158

Modify the import files' storage location 159

Organize your files into a single Music folder. 159

Convert audio file types in Mac Music 159

Adjust the music settings 160

Chapter 17..161

Family and friends 161

Setup your Macbook Family Sharing 161

Configure a child's screen time on a Mac 163

Set Screen Time on Mac to impose privacy and
content limitations 164

Utilize Screen Time on Mac to schedule downtime
....166

Create a downtime schedule. 167

Activate or deactivate the downtime schedule 168

Immediately turn downtime on or off.................169

Configure Communication Safety in Mac Screen
Time...170

CHAPTER 18...172

Facetime on your Macbook Air 172

Making a video call via Facetime 172

Answering or Taking a FaceTime video call 172

Turn down a FaceTime video chat 173

Stop or Close a FaceTime video chat.....................173

Use your Macbook to make & receive group
FaceTime calls 174

Launch a fresh FaceTime group chat 174

Include extra participants in a FaceTime video chat
....174

Adding additional participants to an audio
FaceTime call 175

Answering or Taking a FaceTime group call.........175

Reject a FaceTime group video call 176

Pausing or muting a group FaceTime video call
....176

Joining a FaceTime call on your Mac via a link....176

CHAPTER 19 177

Privacy and security 177

Use Your Screen Time 177

Make use of Safari's privacy features. 177

Browse secretly using Mac Safari.......................177

Browse once secretly..178

Always surf in privacy..178

Quit using private browsing. 178

Clear your browser history.................................179

Utilize Mail Privacy Protection 179

Adjust Mail's privacy settings on a Mac 179

Block or unblock senders on your mail.............180

Blocking senders..180

Unblocking blocked senders. 180

Use Mail on a Mac to Hide My Email...................180

Send an email with a special, arbitrary address.
....180

Restrict whoever has access to your Macbook
camera...181

Log in to your Mac using Apple Sign 182

Create an account from an application or a web
page 182

Log in to your account from an internet site or
application 183

Modify the Apple settings for a website or app's
sign-in 183

Configure your Mac to be safe. 183

Configure your Mac to log out when not in use.
....184

Safeguard your data..........................184

Creating a pass key..........................185

Use a passkey to access an account on your Mac.
....185

Set up iCloud Keychain..........................185

Apple ID two-factor authentication 186

Activate two-factor verification on your Apple ID
....186

Utilize two-factor authentication to log in and
obtain a verification code.........................187

CHAPTER 20..........................188

Using find MY..........................188

Configure Find My on a Mac..........................188

Activate the location services. 188

Activate Find My Mac..........................188

Find a device on a Mac by using Find My 189

See the location of a gadget.........................189

Search for a gadget location.........................190

Receiving an alert once a gadget is found.........190

Use iCloud.com's Find Devices feature to find a
device. 190

Find your gadget..........................190

Mark a gadget as lost on Mac..........................191

Verify the whereabouts of a reported missing
device..191

Modify the missing device's message..................192

Toggle between AirTag and other items in Find My on Mac's Lost Mode 192

How is an item protected by Lost Mode?..........192

Activate Lost Mode 192

Modify the phone number displayed in the Lost Mode alert. 193

Disable your AirTags or any item's Lost Mode in Find My on Mac 193

Disable Mark as Lost in Mac Find My..............193

View item details on a Mac in Find My 194

Personalize find MY 194

View your present location. 194

Look at a 3D map..194

CHAPTER 21..195

Printing documents via your Macbook printer........195

Select a paper size for your printed document on Mac 196

Modifying the size (dimension) of the printing paper 196

Modify the default paper size that you usually print on. 197

CHAPTER 22 198

Troubleshooting common problems.....................198

How to Fix a Mac That Doesn't Power Off 198

Backing up your Macbook 199

Pair a storage device with a Macbook................199

Connecting the Drive 199

Formatting a New Drive 201

Configure the storage media as a backup disc..203

Making your device back up 204

Utilize a backup to reinstate your Macbook 204

Use Migration Assistant 205

Book index...209

Introduction

With the release of the new MacBook Air with the powerful M3 CPU today, Apple has elevated its already remarkable blend of mobility and power-efficient performance to a whole new level. With the M3 chip, the MacBook Air can operate up to 60% quicker than the M1 model and up to 13 times faster than the quickest MacBook Air with an Intel processor.1. And the MacBook Air remains the greatest consumer laptop for AI in the world because to its quicker and more effective Neural Engine in the M3. The 13- and 15-inch MacBook Air have similar features, including an amazing Liquid Retina display, up to 18 hours of battery life, and additional capabilities, including two times faster Wi-Fi than the previous model and capability for two external screens. The new MacBook Air comes in four stunning colors: space grey, silver, and midnight, which has a revolutionary anodization finish to prevent fingerprints, and starlight. Its sturdy aluminum unibody enclosure is made to last. The MacBook Air offers an unparalleled experience because of its superior camera, microphones, and speakers; MagSafe charging; silent, fanless design; and macOS. As a result, the 13-inch model is the best-selling laptop globally, while the 15-inch variant is the best-selling laptop globally.

MacBook Air (13- & 15-inch) Specifications

S/N	Features	Spec
1	Display size	13- & 15-inch
2	CPU and GPU	8-core CPU and 10-core GPU
3	Chip	M3
4	Storage	256GB SSD expandable to 512GB, 1TB, or 2TB
5	memory	Up to 24GB
6		
7	Ports	2 Thunderbolt / USB 4
8	Camera	1080p FaceTime HD camera
9	Battery	18 hours of battery life
10	Price	Entry price at $1,099

Additional features and what to expect

1. Versatile design with two ideal sizes for portability: The 13- and 15-inch MacBook Air have an amazing battery life, are exceptionally light, and are less than half an inch thin, making it possible for users to work, play, or create from anywhere thanks to their long-lasting aluminum in closure. While the 15-inch variant gives even more screen real estate for multitasking, the 13-inch size delivers the best mobility.

2. Stunning Liquid Retina display: The MacBook Air has a 13.6- or 15.3-inch Liquid Retina display that supports 1 billion colors, has a brightness of up to 500 nits

3. Support for two external displays: The MacBook Air with M3 can now accommodate two external monitors while the laptop lid is closed. This feature is ideal for business users or anybody who needs multiple screens to spread out papers or multitask between program

4. Adaptable connectivity: Wi-Fi 6E, which offers download rates up to twice as fast as the previous generation, is included with the MacBook Air with M3.

5. Camera, microphones, and speakers: Users can look their best whether collaborating with colleagues worldwide or interacting with friends and family thanks to the 1080p FaceTime HD camera. With a three-mic array and improved speech quality during audio and video chats, users will also sound their best. Dolby Atmos and Spatial Audio are supported by the MacBook Air's immersive sound system, which enables users to enjoy three-dimensional soundstages for movies and music.

6. Magic Keyboard with Touch ID: With the touch of a finger, users can quickly, easily, and securely unlock their Mac, log in to applications and websites, and make payments using Apple Pay. The Magic Keyboard is a silent, ergonomic backlit keyboard that boasts a full-height function row.

7. macOS Sonoma: Now, users may arrange widgets directly on the desktop, click to interact with them, and even use the MacBook Air to access the vast ecosystem of iPhone widgets. Excellent features like Presenter Overlay and Reactions make video conferences more interesting. Web applications offer

quicker access to favorite websites, while Safari profiles keep surfing distinct between various topics or projects. And with Game Mode, gaming is much more enjoyable.

8. Increased productivity: With compatibility for up to two external monitors, users—including business professionals—can make use of the MacBook Air's large display with Split View or spread out across screens. Users such as students are also assisted in maintaining concentration on the job at hand by features such as Stage Manager.

9. Extensive application selection: The MacBook Air boasts an impressive collection of pre-installed applications, like as FaceTime, Freeform, iMovie, GarageBand, and Photos, in addition to productivity tools like Pages, Numbers, and Keynote, which let people accomplish excellent work with ease. Additionally, all of the popular programs on macOS, such as Microsoft 365 and other beloved iOS apps, operate very quickly because of the hundreds of apps that have been tailored for Apple hardware.

10. The pricing starts at $999 for the 13-inch, while the 15-inch with M3 starts at $1,199 (US)

Chapter 1

Upgrading to the new macOS Sonoma

The first thing we will be taking you through in this book guide is to download and install the new macOS Sonoma into your Macbook

Firstly check out if your gadget is compatible with the new macOS Sonoma below

Check out which device is Compatible with the new macOS 14

- iMac: 2019 & the recent
- 2017 iMac Pro
- MacBook Air: (2018) & recent
- The 2018 Macbook Air
- Mac Pro: 2019 & recent
- Mac Studio: 2022 & recent
- Mac Mini: 2018 & recent

Check if macOs Sonoma can work on your Mac

you may determine whether or not your Mac supports macOS 14 via

1. Navigate to Apple ID >

2. Hit on About this Mac and
3. See or verify the aforesaid segment to view it.

Downloading & installing the new macOS Sonoma

Utilize Software (upgrade) Update to install the newest current edition (model) of macOS Sonoma. It may take less disc room storage to download & install, and it's the quickest and most straightforward method of getting macOS updates. (check out the use software update at the end of this chapter)

- Select System Settings via the Apple menu that appears at the angle of your display screen. In the sidebar, select General. now, touch or pick the Software Update via the right-hand corner.

- Alternatively, select Software Update via the menu logo> System preference in previous iterations of macOS.

- Alternatively, search for "Software Update" utilizing Spotlight via your menu icon and choose it from the list of results.

If Software Update isn't available on your older Mac, you can search the App Store for macOS Sonoma.

Alternatively

From the provided URL below, you may download every version of macOS 14 Sonoma that has been made available. In the link in your browser to install the latest macOS

- UniversalMac_14.0_23A5257q_Restore.ipsw

Once you have been able to download the new software, the next step is to install it into your device, follow the prompt below to do so

Installing Mac OS X Sonoma

For macOS Ventura or recent

1. Navigate to and touch System setup> General > Touch Software Update
2. Next, choose the information icon next to the Beta updates
3. Next, pick the developer beta for macOS Sonoma
4. Immediately download and install this update on your Mac
5. You might use the Software Update page to install further updates.

For macOS 13.3 Ventura or earlier models

1. Download & configure the aforesaid new macOS Beta Access Utility
2. After that, run it and follow the installation instructions that appear on the screen
3. You might use the Software Update page to install further updates.

Set up macOS 14

1. Ensure that you are using the most recent version of macOS 13.4 Ventura

2. Then click on Info next to Beta Updates in System Setups > General

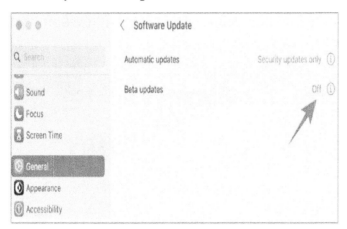

3. Next, click the Done button next to macOS Sonomo Beta Updates

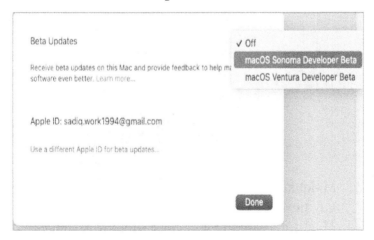

4. The download and installation will now take place. Restart your Mac after you're done.

To get the newest version of macOS Sonoma on your Mac and install it, follow these instructions.

Your macOS software Update to the newest version

To install updates and upgrades for macOS and its pre-installed applications, such as Safari, use Software Update.

Using software updates

1. Make a backup of your Mac before installing any new software. You may utilize Time Machine to create a backup of your Mac by using an exterior storage space tool.

2. Open Software Update to see if there is any new software available.

   - Select System Settings via the Apple menu logo located at the angle of your display screen. In the sidebar, select General. Now, hit on or select Software Update via the rightward angle.

   - Alternatively, select Software Update via the Apple menu logo > System Preferences in previous iterations of macOS.

3. Touch the Upgrade (update) option to install any updated software that Software Update detects. Your administrator passphrase, used to access your Mac, will need to be entered. Your Macbook will exhibit a blank screen or progress bar many times during the installation process. There isn't any new software accessible for your Macbook version right now if Software Update indicates that your Mac is up to date. Software Update displays only software that is compatible with MacBook models.

Should the Software Update not appear

   - Via the event that System Setups or System Preference do not include a Software Update option, click the Spotlight symbol in the bottom left angle of your display screen and type Software Update into the search bar. You can get the Software Update from the search results if it is located.

- Use the App Store in place of Software Update if your earlier Mac does not have it. try to view via the folder Apps. To find updates, touch the Updates logo in the Application Store or perform a name-based search for the app.

Chapter 2

Turn on or off your MacBook gadget

Toggle on your device

1. Hit on the control knob on your Macbook or hit on Bar's rightward to halt awaiting once the monitor toggle on & exhibits the sign-in bar.

Toggle your Macbook off

1. Hit Shut Downward by hitting the Apple emblem in the upper section leftward angle of the display

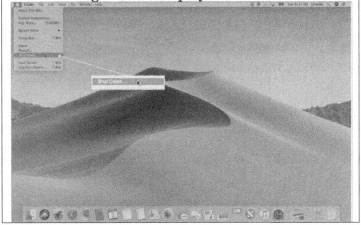

Restarting your device after installation or upgrade

1. Select the Apple icon menu > Restart on your Mac.

   - De-select "Reopen windows when logging back in" if you don't want to open program windows to reopen once your Macbook starts all over.

Charging your Macbook battery

Every time your Macbook Air is powered on, the battery recharges

Charge the battery

Pair your MacBook Air with a power source using the included connector and power adapter.

Exhibit the battery percentage via the menu bar.

1. Click Control Centre in System Settings, then

2. Select Battery on the right, and lastly

3. Click Show in the Menu Bar.

The menu bar offers the option to display the battery % as well.

Adjust the battery settings.

System Settings is where you may adjust many battery-related settings.

Optimize or Enhance Battery Charging

To enable Optimized Battery Charging,

1. Navigate to System Settings,

2. Choose Battery from the flank-bar,

3. Touch the information icon after Battery Health.

Low Power Mode

1. Touch the battery in the sidebar of System Settings.

2. Select the desired choice from the Low Power Mode pop-up menu

High Power Mode

1. touch Battery in the flank-bar of System Settings, and then

2. Select an item from the High Power Mode selection.

View the battery-charged level

To view the battery level or charging status,

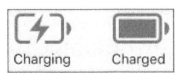

- Look at the battery status symbol located at the right of the menu bar. Alternatively,

- Choose Battery via the flank bar of System Settings.

Battery life history

To view the battery usage for the previous 10 days or the last 24 hours,

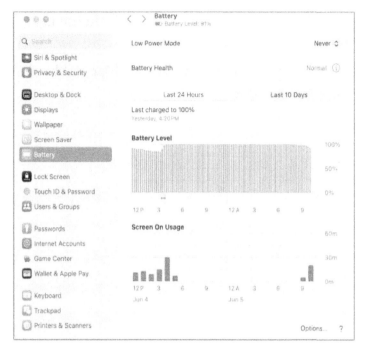

- navigate to System setup (Settings) &

- Select Battery.

Reduce battery consumption.

You may decrease the brightness of the display, shut down programs, and unplug unused minimized applications to increase the amount of time your battery lasts on a single charge. To adjust your power settings,

1. Select Battery from the sidebar of System Settings. The device's battery may discharge if your Macbook Air is sleeping while another device is attached to it.

Once you have been able to toggle on or restart your gadget, the next important thing to do is to set it up, this will be explained comprehensively in the next chapter

This setup works for both new and older Macbook Air and Air users

Chapter 3

Setup your new Macbook Air

You will be able to move data via a different PC, set up Touch ID, and tweak key Mac settings once you set up your latest Macbook Air. To configure your fresh band new Macbook faster, you may also be able to skip a few steps and use your current settings if you already own a Mac

Set or configure your Macbook Air for first-time Mac users

Before starting this

- o   During setup, have your iPad or iPhone handy, since some stages might need confirmation on a different device

- o   During setup, you will be given the preference to move data via a different PC, such as a Windows PC. Make sure the machine you wish to transfer data from has the most recent software version installed on it before you do this.

- o   Your Macbook Air may be easily configured with Setup Assistant, and it shouldn't take long to finish. Set aside more time, though, if you decide to move data.

1. **Setting your preferred language, nation, or area, then establish a Wi-Fi connection.**

   o Select a language. Your Mac's language is set by doing this. Later on, to modify the language, go to System Settings, select Language & Region from the sidebar, and then make your selections.

   o Select your nation or area. This configures your Mac's date format, currency, temperature, and other settings. Open System Settings, select General from the sidebar, click Language & Region, and then make your selections

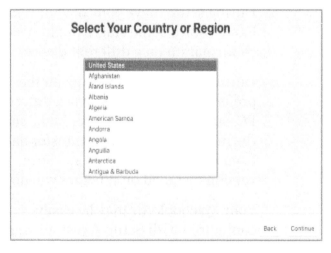

   o Activate the accessibility options. Click Not Now to view accessibility choices for motor, hearing, vision, and cognitive abilities. Press the Escape key on your keyboard to configure VoiceOver on your Mac. To see more accessibility choices, you may also triple-click Touch ID, which is the top right button on your keyboard

o Pair to or Join a wireless network. Select your Wi-Fi network and, if required, enter the password. You may also choose Other Network Options and follow the onscreen instructions if you're using Ethernet.

o Open System Settings, select Wi-Fi from the sidebar, select a network, and if required, enter the password to modify the Wi-Fi network later.

2. **Transferring data via a PC to a different one**

o You may transfer all of your data from a Windows computer to your new Mac, including files, contacts, accounts, and more.

o Before starting. Make sure the software on your Windows computer is updated to the most recent version. Then, on your Windows computer, download Migration Assistant.

o Wi-Fi data transfer is used. You need to connect your new Mac and Windows computer to the same wireless network. On the setup screen, click your Windows computer, then adhere to the prompts.

o Utilizing an Ethernet wire, move data. Use an Ethernet cable to connect your Mac directly to your Windows computer.

o Depending on its ports, you might want an adaptor to connect the Ethernet connection to your Windows computer. Once they are connected, click your Windows computer to see the setup page, then adhere to the prompts.

o **Making the data transfer later.** You can also decide not to send any data at all at this moment. If so, in the Migration Assistant Window, choose Not Now. After setup, to move data,

3. **Create an account on your computer and log in using your Apple ID.**

   o Using your Apple ID, log in. You probably already have an Apple ID if you own another Apple product, such as an iPad or iPhone. You may create a free Apple ID right now if you don't already have one

   o If you have an Apple ID, sign in using your password and email address. An iPhone or iPad that you own will receive a verification code. A verification code is texted to the phone number linked to your Apple ID if you don't own an iPhone or iPad. Follow the on-screen instructions if you don't get the text or the verification code

   o Touch "generate new or fresh Apple ID" if not have any yet

   o If your password or Apple ID is lost: Select "Forgot password or Apple ID."

   o Click Set Up Later if you would prefer not to create or sign in with an Apple ID at this time. Following setup, you may use your existing Apple ID to log in or create a new one. Click "Sign in with your Apple ID" in the sidebar after opening System Settings.

- **Create or generate an account on the PC.**

Create an account by adding your name and creating a password. This password may be used to unlock your Mac and authorize other actions. If you can't remember your computer account password, you can include an optional clue to assist you in getting it back. Click it to change your account's login image, then select an alternative.

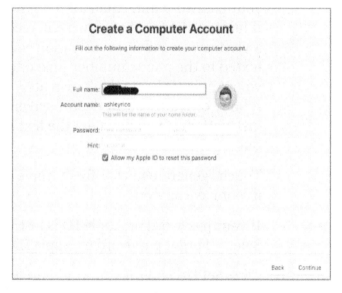

Create a Computer Account

Fill out the following information to create your computer account.

Full name:

Account name: ashleyrico

This will be the name of your home folder.

Password:

Hint:

☑ Allow my Apple ID to reset this password

Back   Continue

- However, if you tick this option during setup, you may use your Apple ID to reset the password if you ever forget the one to unlock your Mac. Note: Your computer account and Apple ID are not the same.

4. Set this as your primary (new) Mac

- By utilizing the settings from your iCloud account, you may utilize Make This Your New Mac without having to go through multiple setup processes. Click Continue to utilize your existing settings. Setting up the Touch & Apple Pay ID is the next step in the setup procedure.

- Click Customize Settings and move on to the next step if you want to change the settings on your brand-new Macbook Air.

5. Personalize and adjust the privacy and security settings on your Mac, activate Screen Time, and make Siri available

- Give Location Services a go. Select whether to let location-aware programs on your Mac, such as Maps. Later, enter System Settings, select Privacy & Security from the sidebar, click Location Services, and make your selections. This will allow you to modify your Location Services settings

- You receive a screen where you may select your time zone if you don't activate Location Services.

- Give developers and Apple access to your analytics. Select whether to allow

Apple to share crashes and use statistics with developers, as well as whether to transmit diagnostics and data to Apple. Open System Settings, select Privacy & Security from the sidebar, then Analytics & Improvements (you might have to scroll), and select an option to modify these settings later.

o Configure Screen Time. Via Screen Time, you will be able to monitor the amount of period you expend on your Macbook Air every day and each week, regulate your kids' screen time, and set time limitations for certain applications. Click Continue to switch it on; click Set Up Later to turn it off. To select your options if you decide to set up later, enter System Settings and select Screen Time from the sidebar

o Use FileVault to protect your files. FileVault adds to the safety of your info. You have the option to enable your iCloud account to unlock your disc if you forget your password, as well as to enable FileVault to safeguard your data during setup.

o **Turn on Siri and say "Hey Siri."** During setup, you may activate Siri and say "Hey Siri" to make your requests audible. Click Enable Ask Siri to get started with Siri. When asked, say several Siri instructions to set up "Hey

Siri." Later, enter System Settings, select Siri & Spotlight from the sidebar, and make your selections to activate Siri and say "Hello Siri."

- o To make Siri better during setup, you may also decide to share audio with Apple. Later on, you may always decide not to share the audio. Navigate to Privacy & Safety in the side or flank-bar of System Settings, choose Analytics & Improvements (you might have to scroll), and make your selections.

6. Setup Apple Pay & Touch ID

- o Configure Touch ID. During setup, you may add a fingerprint to Touch ID (the top-right button on your keyboard), which you can use to sign into some third-party applications, unlock your Macbook Air, and approve transactions using Apple Pay. To set the Touch ID, follow the onscreen prompts

- o Configure Apple Pay. In addition to adding a debit, credit, or store card that may be used to make Touch ID purchases, setting up Touch ID also allows you to add Apple (Pay). Input your card information and adhere to the on-screen instructions. You may be asked to validate this card first if you currently utilize it to generate media purchases.

o   Hit on Apple & Wallet (Pay) in System Settings to configure Apple Pay or add more cards later. Observe the on-screen instructions to configure Apple Pay.

7. personalize the desktop form

o   Decide on your style. You may pick via Light, shady, or Auto for your desktop theme. Later, visit System Settings, click Appearance, and choose an option if you wish to reverse the setting decision you made. Other visual options, including sidebar icon size and highlight color, are also configurable.

o   **Finish Setup.** The new Macbook Air is prepared for use

Chapter 4

Knowing simple Gestures

Simple trackpad gestures on your new Macbook gadget

With your Macbook Air, you will be able to do lots of stuff with basic trackpad motions and gestures.

1. **Click:** Use the trackpad's & click anyplace. Alternatively,
   * Go to Trackpad Settings,
   * Activate "Tap to click," and
   * Just tap.
2. **Force click**:
   * Press down after clicking
3. **Secondary click, or right-click:**
   * in this case: Use two fingers to click to bring up shortcut menus. When "Tap to click" is on, use two fingers to tap.
   * Click the trackpad and hit the Control knob on the keyboard.
4. **Scroll using two fingers**:
   * Via sliding 2 of your fingers upward or downward
5. **To be able to zoom in/out of**

pictures and web pages
- Squeeze your thumb & touch
- Then open or close it while still in the printed form.

6. **Swipe to navigate:**
   - Use two fingers to slide leftward or rightward to move between webpages, documents, and more like flipping a page in a book.

7. **Launchpad:** Launchpad allows you to open apps quickly.
   - Use four or five fingers to pinch closed, and then
   - touch an application to launch it.

8. **Swipe between applications:**
   - Use three or four fingers to swipe left or right to move between full-screen apps.

CHAPTER 5

Managing and setting up Apple ID on a Mac

1. Open the Apple menu on your Mac, select System Settings, and then hit or touch [your designation] in the sidebar at the top

    o If you dont see your name, select "Sign in with your Apple ID," input your passphrase, trailed by your Apple ID (or accessible At mail info or handset digit number you provided in the Apple ID settings). You will be able to create or generate an Apple ID if not having any yet

2. To adjust the relevant Apple ID setups on your Macbook, hit on one of the subsequent things on the right:

   o   Personal or Individual Data

   o   Security & Sign-In

   o   Shipping and payment:

   o   iCloud:

   o   Buying (purchase) & Media:

   o   Family Sharing:

   o   Gadgets (devices)

   o   Signing Out

   o   Privacy & Apple ID Information

Creating or generating an Apple ID on your Macbook Air

Using your current email address or a randomly created iCloud email address, you may create an Apple ID on your Mac.

1. From the Apple menu in System setup on your Macbook, select "Sign in with your Apple ID" from the sidebar's top drop-down menu

2. Click **Not having a User Account**, then adhere to the directions displayed on the screen.

Configure your Apple ID's data on a Mac

You may modify the Apple ID-related picture, designation, & birthday using the Personal Information settings.

1. Pick the Apple icon menu > System Setups on your Macbook, and then select [your name] in the sidebar at the top.

   o If you don't see your name, select "Sign in with your Apple ID," input your passphrase, trailed by your Apple ID (or accessible At mail info or handset digit number you provided in the Apple ID settings). You will be able to create or generate an Apple ID if not having any yet

2. On the right, click Personal Information, and then examine or modify the following:

   o Monogram, picture, or memento

   o Date of birth

   o Choosing a Communication Style

Set up your Mac's Apple ID sign-in and security details

You may modify the mail, handset digit numbers, & security setups linked to your Apple ID using the log-in & safety Settings app.

1. Open the Apple menu on your Mac, select System Settings, and then hit [your designation] in the sidebar at the top.

   o If you don't see your name, select "Sign in with your Apple ID," type your password, followed by your Apple logo ID (or accessible mail info or handset digit number you provided in the Apple ID settings). You may now create or generate an Apple ID if you not having any yet

2. On the right, choose Sign-In & Security. Then, inspect or modify the following:

Set up your Apple ID mailing address and payment method on Mac

The payment and shipping details linked to your Apple ID can be changed using the Apple ID Payment and Shipping options.

1. Open the Apple menu on your Mac, select System Settings, and then hit or touch [your designation] in the sidebar at the top

2. On the right, click Payment and Shipping. Then, view or modify any of the subsequent(shown options)

Organize your Apple ID's media and buying preferences on a Mac

1. Open the Apple menu on your Mac, select System Settings, and then hit on Touch [your designation] in the sidebar at the top

2. On the right, choose Media & Purchases

3. Execute any of the subsequent(shown options)

Log in or out of your Apple ID on a Mac

Login with your Apple ID

1. From the Apple menu in System Setups on your Mac, select "Sign in with your Apple ID" from the sidebar's top drop-down menu

   o If your name appears, you are already logged in.

2. Type your Apple ID (or another Reachable At email or phone number you provided in the Apple ID setups), and now hit Continue

3. After entering your password and clicking Continue, proceed as directed on the page.

Signing out or Exiting your Apple ID

1. Open the Apple menu on your Mac, select System Settings, and then hit or touch [your designation] in the sidebar at the top

2. On the right, click Sign Out

3. To copy and download your iCloud data, follow the on-screen instructions.

CHAPTER 6

APPLE PAY

Use Apple Pay on Your Mac and Set It Up

You may use the Touch ID sensor on your MacBook Air or MacBook Pro to approve Apple Pay transactions on your Mac.

How to Configure Apple Pay in Mac Safari

When using Apple's Safari on a Mac, you must be making online payments.

1. Launch Safari
2. Via the menu bar, hit on Safari -> options.
3. Select the Privacy tab.

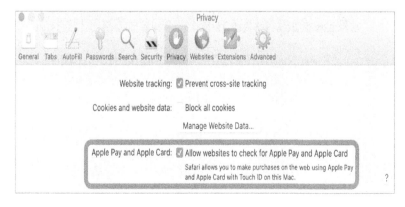

4. To allow websites to verify if Apple Pay is configured, tick the option next to Apple Pay.

Configure Touch ID with Apple Pay on a MacBook

You can approve Apple Pay transactions using your keyboard if your MacBook Air or MacBook Pro has a Touch ID sensor.

However, you must first have linked a credit card to your Mac's Apple Pay list before you can proceed. When you first set up a MacBook Air or MacBook Pro with a Touch ID sensor, you are prompted to do this; however, you may also add a card to Apple Pay at any time by going into System Preferences.

1. Open System Preferences using the Apple menu bar (□BOX -> System Preferences...), the Applications folder, or the Dock on your Mac
2. To access the appropriate window, click Wallet & Apple Pay.
3. To add a credit or debit card, click Add Card.

Pay

Add credit, debit, or store cards and use
Apple Pay with Touch ID to make purchases
easily and securely, right from your Mac.

Card-related information, location, device settings, and device
use patterns will be sent to Apple and may be shared together
with account information with your card issuer or bank to set up
Apple Pay.
See how your data is managed...

Add Card...   ?

4. Hold your card in front of your Mac's FaceTime
camera and place it within the screen's frame
to input your card information. You also have
the option to manually enter the card details

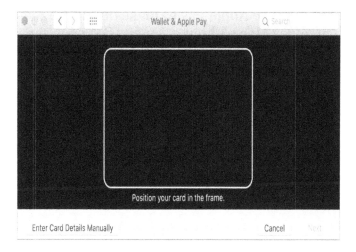

Position your card in the frame.

Enter Card Details Manually   Cancel   Next

5. To confirm your card number, click Next
6. Check the number on your card, then select
Next

7. Use the three-digit CVV or CVC security code displayed on the back of the card to confirm the card's expiration date, then click Next
8. To accept the conditions & rules, hit on Accept
9. Click Next after selecting Email, Text Message, or Call to confirm that your card is configured for Apple Pay.
10. Type in the verification code you received by the method of your choice, then click Next.
11.
12. Apple Pay should now be linked to your card. Your bank may occasionally need some time to check your details; in such case, you will be informed as soon as your card is accepted.

Enable Apple Pay on an earlier Mac

You can still use Apple Pay to make online purchases with an older Mac without a Touch ID sensor, but you'll need to utilize the cards that are saved on your iPhone or Apple Watch. However, you must first turn on a few switches on your gadget (s).

Enable iPhone-Based Apple Pay Payments on a Mac

1. Open the iPhone's Settings app.
2. Select Apple Pay & Wallet

3. Make sure the switch for "Allow Payments on Mac" is in the green "ON" position by tapping it.

Enable Macbook Air Apple Watch Apple Pay Payments

1. Open your iPhone's Watch app
2. Select Apple Pay and Wallet

3. Make sure the switch for "Allow Payments on Mac" is in the green "ON" position by tapping it.

How to Use Your Mac to Manage Apple Pay Cards

In System Preferences, you may manage the cards you've added to Apple Pay if your Mac includes a Touch ID sensor.

1. Open System Preferences using the Apple menu bar (⠿box -> System Preferences...), the Applications folder, or the Dock on your Mac.
2. To access the appropriate window, click Wallet & Apple Pay.
3. In the sidebar, click a card to examine its data, which includes the account number, billing address, bank contact information, and transaction history.

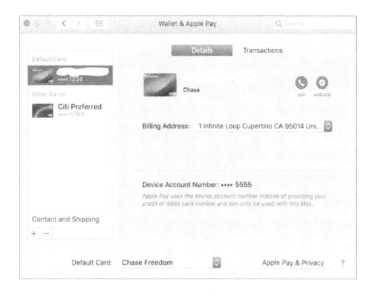

You can only manage your cards on your iPhone if you're using Apple Pay on an older Mac and authorizing transactions with your watch or iPhone.

Modify the Default Apple Pay Card on the Macbook Air

1. Open System Preferences using the Apple menu bar (box -> System Preferences.), the Applications folder, or the Dock on your Mac.
2. Select Apple Pay & Wallet.

3. From the pop-up option labeled "Default Card" located at the bottom of the preference pane, choose your favorite card.

Remove or Take a Card Out of your Mac Apple Pay

1. Open System Preferences using the Apple menu bar (box -> System Preferences), the Applications folder, or the Dock on your Mac.
2. To access the appropriate window, click Wallet & Apple Pay
3. Select the card you want to delete by clicking on it in the sidebar
4. To delete the sidebar, use the minus (-) button located at its bottom.

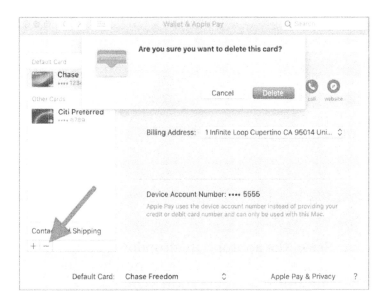

Modify Your Shipping and Contact Detail

1. Open System Preferences using the Apple menu bar (box -> System Preferences...), the Applications folder, or the Dock on your Mac.
2. To access the appropriate window, click Wallet & Apple Pay.
3. Select the Contact and Shipping links located in the sidebar's bottom.

4. Select the appropriate dropdown option to update or add a new phone number, email address, or mailing address.

Adjusting or Modifying Your Billing Address

1. Open System Preferences using the Apple menu bar (box -> System Preferences.), the Applications folder, or the Dock on your Mac.
2. To access the appropriate window, click Wallet & Apple Pay.
3. Select the card whose billing address you want to modify from the sidebar.
4. Hit on the billing info dropdown & click include a fresh billing info

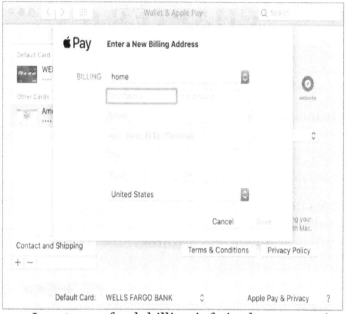

5. Input your fresh billing info in the appropriate box & hit on the save icon

CHAPTER 6

iCloud

Your images, files, and backups are just a few examples of the crucial data that iCloud enables you to keep safe, current, and accessible across every one of your gadgets.

A free email address and 5 GB of data storage are both included with iCloud. You may subscribe to iCloud+ for greater storage and features.

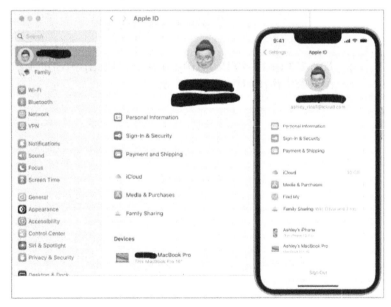

Storing folders in iCloud Drive on Mac

You may securely save any sort of document in iCloud using iCloud Drive, and you can view it from any of your devices as well as online at iCloud.com.

Configure iCloud Drive

You may now configure iCloud settings to set iCloud Drive on this Mac if you haven't already.

1. Open the Apple icon menu on your Mac, select System Settings, and then hit or touch [your designation] in the sidebar at the top.

2. Toggle on Synchronize this Macbook, then select iCloud via the rightward section, followed by iCloud Drive

3. Press "Done."

Keep your Documents and Desktop folders on iCloud Drive

1. Select System Preferences from the Apple icon menu on your Mac, then select [your name] in the sidebar's upper section

2. Select iCloud from the menu via the rightward section, then select iCloud Drive. Confirm that iCloud Drive is toggled on or activated

3. Activate the Documents & Desktop Folders

4. Select "Done."

Collaborate & share folders using iCloud

To work together on projects, you may share folders and files using iCloud Drive with other people.

Allow individuals to work together in folders

1. On your Mac, use any of the subsequent proceedings to invite others to collaborate on folders:

   o After opening a Finder window by clicking the Dock's Finder icon, choose a folder from the sidebar by clicking iCloud Drive, and then hit the Share button

   o To share an object on the desktop, control-click it and select it via the shortcut option.

Note: A folder has to be in iCloud (Drive) for others to work on it with you.

2. Select Collaborate from the option that appears

3. Below "just invited individual will be able to edit," hit on the URL. Work together to create group permissions, then select one of the options from the drop-down menu labeled "Who can access" below:

4. A pop-up menu beneath Permissions will be exhibited; Touch one of the following onscreen directives:

5. To enable sharing of the folder with other people, tick the box next to "Allow others to invite." To limit who may share the folder with others, UNCHECK the checkbox

6. You may either make & duplicate a URL to the shared stuff or distribute the invitation via Mail or Messages.

Accept a file or folder-sharing invitation

A folder that you share can have its sharing parameters changed at any moment.

1. To access iCloud Drive on your Macbook, hit on the Finder logo on the Dock to launch a Finder window, and then choose it from the sidebar

2. Select Manage Shared File or Manage Shared Folder by performing a control-click on the file or folder.

3. Take action with any of the popped-up directives

4. Select "Done."

See and control the files you've shared

To quickly browse files and folders that you and other people have shared, utilize the Shared folder in the Finder sidebar. Follow these steps to configure your shared folder so that the folders are arranged according to who shared them:

1. To launch a Finder window via your Macbook, hit on the Finder logo on the Dock. on the sidebar, select Shared

2. Select Shared By from the Grouping pop-up box that appears in the toolbar.

The shared files and folders between you and other users are shown in the pane, arranged according to who shared them first.

Quit sharing a folder

1. Hit on the Finder logo on the Dock to launch a Finder window, now select iCloud Drive from the sidebar to access it on your Mac
2. Control-click the item to select Manage Shared File or Manage Shared Folder
3. Trail any of the directives that emerge:
   - To halt sharing with every person, hit on "Stop Sharing".
   - Give up sharing with a precise individual: drag the indicator above the name of the person, click, and choose Remove Access.

View and manage the storage on your iCloud

1. Via your Mac, choose System Preferences from the Apple menu, then click [your name] in the upper portion of the sidebar
2. From the iCloud menu on the right, choose Manage. Then, try any of the following:

   o Invest in better storage:

- Talk about iCloud+ with your relatives:
- Examine how a feature or program uses storage:
- Take out a backup of an iOS or iPad-OS device:
- Switch off Siri and erase any data connected to it:

1. Select "Done."

Utilize Mac iCloud Photos

All of the images & movies in your picture library are saved in iCloud with iCloud Photos, allowing you to view them from iCloud.com as well as your Macbook

Before to beginning

1. Verify that the software on your Macbook & other gadgets is up to date

2. To sign in, utilize your Apple ID:

Activate iCloud Pictures.

1. Select Photos > Settings from within the Pictures application on your Macbook, & then select iCloud

2. Click the checkbox for iCloud Photos

3. Pick one of the subsequent choices:

Install Originals on This Mac: Make the Most of Mac Storage

Stop utilizing iCloud Pictures on your Mac

To prevent photo updates between your Macbook & other gadgets, you may disable iCloud Photos on your Mac.

1. Select Photos > Settings from within the Pictures application on your Macbook, & then select iCloud.

2. Uncheck the option next to iCloud Photos

3. Select Download to start downloading images and movies via iCloud to your Macbook, or select Take Out via Macbook to get rid of any partially downloaded files.

Your photo library stays in iCloud and is accessible to your other devices that utilize iCloud Photos even after you switch off iCloud Pictures on your Mac.

Stop using iCloud Pictures on all Apple laptops and gadgets

1. Select System Preferences from the Apple menu via your Macbook, now hit on [your name] in the sidebar's upper section

2. Click "Sign in with your Apple ID" to sign in or establish an Apple ID if you are not able to view your name.

• Toggle between iCloud and the right.

3. Select Photos from the Manage menu, then select "Turn Off and Delete.

Chapter 7

Pairing or Link your Macbook Air computer to the internet

Utilize WiFi

Pair to an available WiFi network

1. On your Mac, select the network you wish to join by clicking the Wi-Fi icon via the menu bar logo.

   • Hit on Other (services) Networks to view neighboring networks if you are unable to find the network you wish to join.

2. Click Join after entering the network password if prompted.

Connect to a secret WiFi network

To join a secret network, you have to understand its name, password, and security protocol.

1. On your Mac, select Other Networks from the menu bar by clicking the Wi-Fi icon, and then select Other from the list of Other Networks at the bottom

2. Fill in the service designation field with the designation of the wireless service

3. Select the kind of wireless security the network employs by clicking the Security pop-up menu

4. Click Join after providing the data for any further forms that appear, such as a username and password.

Utilize Ethernet to pair your Mac to the web

1. To connect your computer's Ethernet haven to a modem or other network device (such as a switch or router), use an Ethernet cable. Use a USB to Ethernet or adapter if your computer lacks an Ethernet connector

2. Select System Preferences via the Apple menu on your Mac, then select Network in the sidebar. You be required to navigate downward

3. Select the Ethernet service on the right, and then select Details

4. You may choose to enable or disable Limit IP infos track

5. Select your ISP's suggested configuration method by clicking TCP or IP in the sidebar, selecting Configure IPv4 from the pop-up menu, and then clicking OK

6. To change the search domain settings or change the DNS server, hit on DNS in the sidebar and input the information you got

7. To access Windows web designationService, touch the **WINS** logo. in the sidebar and input the credentials you were sent if you were given WINS settings

8. If the proxy server settings were sent to you, hit Proxy via the side or flank bar and input the details

9. Click Hardware on the sidebar and input the details you were given if you were sent Ethernet hardware settings

10. Press OK.

Utilize the Instant Hotspot

Make a Wi-Fi connection.

1. Verify that the Apple ID you use to log in on your Mac and iOS or iPadOS device is the same

2. Select your ios or iPad on your Mac by clicking the Wi-Fi status symbol in the menu bar

   o Once your iOS or iPad is connected to a personal hotspot, you can check the battery life and cellular signal strength of your device using the Wi-Fi status menu.

   o To preserve battery life, your devices will automatically disconnect when you're not using the hotspot.

Use USB to connect.

1. Use the USB cord that came with your device to connect your ios or iPad to your Mac

2. Tap Trust if you get an alert on your iOS or iPad that asks you to "Trust This Computer."

View the status of your USB connection and configure it.

1. Select System Preference via the Apple logo menu on your Mac, then select Network in the sidebar. (You will be required to navigate downward.)

2. On the right, choose [your device USB], and then select Details

3. Take any of the following actions, if desired:

   o Examine and configure the USB connection

   o Select System Preference via the Apple logo menu on your Mac, then select Network on the side or flank-bar. (You be required to navigate downward.)

   o On the right, choose [your device USB], and then select Details.

4. Take any of the following actions, if desired:

Use Quick Look to view and edit files on a Mac.

Almost any type of file may be quickly and fully seen without opening it using Quick Look. Within the fast

Look window, you may easily rotate photographs, cut audio and video recordings, and utilize Markup.

1. On your Mac, click the Space bar after selecting one or more things.

   o A window for Quick Look opens. The final thing you choose is displayed first if you picked more than one.

2. Take any of the subsequent proceedings in the Quick Look window:

   o To adjust the window's size, drag its corners. Alternately, use the Full-Screen option located in the Quick or Fast Look window's upper left corner. Click the Exit Full-Screen button that displays after shifting the pointer to the lower section of the window to end full-screen mode.

   o Zooming in or out of an object, use Command-Plus (+) to enlarge the picture or Command-Minus (−) to reduce it.

   o To rotate an object, hit & hold the Option knob (key), now, the Rotate Leftward knob, or hit on the Rotate Rightward button. To keep the thing revolving, click again.

   o Mark up a folder: Press the Markup icon.

o To trim a piece of audio or video, hit on the Trim knob & drag the trimming bar's yellow handles. Click Play to see how your changes look. Click Revert to start afresh. When you're prepared to save your modifications, select whether to overwrite the current file or generate a new one by clicking Done.

o Examine the objects (should you have chosen more than one): Press the Left or Right Arrow keys, or use the arrows located in the upper-left corner of the window. To view the items as a slideshow, click the Play button to watch them in full screen.

o If more than one item was selected, display the items in a grid: Use the Command-Return key or click the Index Sheet button.

o Open an item: Select [App] for Open with.

o Share a product: After selecting the method of sharing the item, click the Share button.

o Copy the topic of an item: You may detach the subject of a photo via the backdrop if the item is a screenshot or snapshot. Control-click on the picture and choose Copy Subject. The subject may now be pasted into a note, email, text message, or document.

3. To shut the Quick Look window when you're finished, click the shut button or use the Space bar.

Chapter 8

Macbook Air Touch ID & trackpad

Make use of the Mac's trackpad and mouse motions

You can utilize gestures, such as click, touch, squeeze, and swipe, to zoom in on docs, navigate via song or internet, rotate photographs, access Notification Centre, etc, whenever you utilize a trackpad / Magic Mouse with your Macbook.

Trackpad gestures

To click, hit on, slide, & perform other actions on your trackpad, place one or additional fingers on its surface. For instance, you may use two fingers to slide leftward or rightward to navigate via sections in a document.

Select Apple icon menu > System Setups (settings), now select Trackpad in the side or flank-bar to see the trackpad gestures that you may utilize on your Macbook, along with a short video that walks you through each motion. You be required to navigate downward

Within the Trackpad settings, gestures may also be customized or turned off.

Mouse gestures

You may click, hit on, or slide objects on your mouse by placing one or additional fingers on its surface. For instance, you may use one finger to slide leftward or rightward to flip between pages in a document.

Select the Apple icon menu > System setup (Settings), then touch the Mouse side or flank-bar to see the mouse movements that you may utilize on your Macbook, along with a short video that walks you through each gesture.

Gestures can also be customized or turned off under the Mouse options.

Utilize Mac Touch ID

You will be able to utilize Touch ID on your Mac or Magic Keyboard to unlock your computer, approve purchases from iTunes, App Store, and Apple Books, and utilize Apple Pay to make online transactions. Additionally, Touch ID can be utilized to log into some third-party apps.

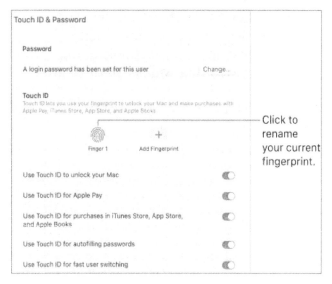

Configure Touch ID.

1. Select System Preference via the Apple logo menu on your Mac, then hit Touch ID & Passphrase on the sidebar.

2. Touch on **Add** Fingerprint & input your passphrase, adhere to the on-screen directions

The Touch ID is situated in the upper right angle of the keyboard if your Macbook or Magic Keyboard has one. Your user account can have close to 3 thumbprints added to it (close to 5 thumbprints saved on your Mac).

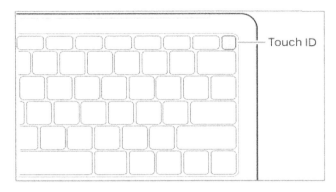

3. Determine how you intend to utilize Touch ID:

- To unlock or open your Macbook after waking it up from sleep, utilize Touch ID.

- Apple Pay: To finish transactions made on this Mac with Apple Pay, utilize Touch ID.

- Apple Books, iTunes Store, and App Store: To finish procurement made on this Macbook from the Apple shops or store, use Touch ID

- Password autofill: When utilizing Safari and other programs, Touch ID can be used to routinely input in user names, passphrases, and credit tag info once prompted

- Quick user switcher: via your Macbook, utilize Touch ID to quickly toggle via user accounts.

Change the name or remove fingerprints

1. Select System Preferences from the Apple menu on your Mac, then hit Touch ID & Passphrase on the sidebar.

2. Utilize any of the following proceedings:

   o To rename a fingerprint, select the text beneath it and type a new name.

   o To remove a fingerprint, select it, type in your password, select Unlock, and finally select Delete.

Utilize Touch ID to open your Macbook, login, or swap users

You must have already entered your password to log into your Mac to utilize Touch ID for these actions.

- Open your Macbok & some passphrase-secured stuff: Simply press and hold Touch ID when prompted to wake your Macbook via sleep or launch a passphrase-protected item.

- Open the login window and log in: Put your thumb on Touch ID after clicking your designation in the sign-in box

- Touch ID unlocks user accounts only those who have passwords. Touch ID is not available to guests or users that are sharing only.

- To switch or toggle users, hit on the menu bar's rapid user switching option, select a new user, and then press your finger to Touch ID

- You must have configured quick user toggling & the user you want to toggle to must have already logged in to the Macbook with a password to utilize Touch ID to toggle to that user.

Utilize Touch ID to generate procurement

1. Input your passphrase to log onto your Mac

2. Buy products via any of the online shops or stores or with Apple Pay

3. When prompted, place your finger on Touch ID.

CHAPTER 9

Stage Manager on Mac

How to Use Mac's Stage Manager

This feels like a big improvement since it makes managing many windows more natural. The instructions below will show you how to utilize Stage Manager on a Mac.

What is a Stage Manager?

With Stage Manager, you may multitask on your Mac or iPad by maintaining one or more windows "center stage" and displaying thumbnails of your open windows at the side of the screen.

You can monitor any changes to those windows without having to open them since the thumbnails are updated. A new program opens or one of the thumbnail windows is clicked to take center stage, turning the open window into a thumbnail. Additionally, groups of several windows that may be opened with a single click can be created.

How to Activate and Deactivate Stage Manager

Turning on and off Stage Manager is a must before you can begin utilizing it. This is a result of the functionality not being turned on by default.

Stage Manager may be enabled or disabled using the Control Centre or System Settings.

To switch Mac System Preferences' Stage Manager on and off:

1. Select System Settings by clicking the Apple symbol.

2. Scroll down the left-hand menu and select Desktop & Dock

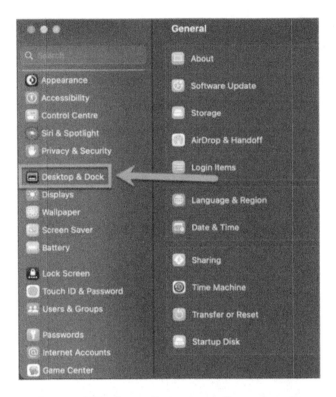

3. Choose Windows & Apps and turn on Stage Manager.

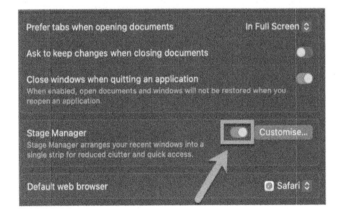

In the Control Centre, to switch Stage Manager on and off:

1. Select the Control Centre menu bar icon.

2. Spot the stage manager's logo. The Stage Manager is in use if it is white. The Stage Manager is not in use if it is grey
3. Tap the symbol to switch between the two states.

You may use Stage Manager as soon as it is switched on. Some thumbnail windows may already be visible on the side of the screen. In addition to letting you navigate between individual application windows, Stage Manager also lets you work with

several windows open within one app and build groups of
applications that open and close simultaneously.

How to Utilize a Single App with Stage Manager

It's easy to go back and forth between the active app
and those that are saved in Stage Manager if you just
want to utilize one app at a time.

**To operate with individual applications in Mac
Stage Manager:**

1. Launch any application. Make sure it's not in
   full-screen mode because Stage Manager won't
   display any full-screen windows
2. Launch an alternative application. Now this
   software is going to take centre stage. To the
   left of the screen will emerge a thumbnail for
   the first application

3. Click the image to return to the original application, and the two will revert to their original positions.

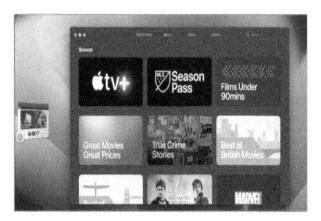

4. Stage Manager will display more thumbnails when more applications are opened. Based on the size of your screen, you can have up to six
5. Older thumbnails will return when you shut more current ones if you open more than your machine can handle.
6. You may also minimize an app to shift it to the side; in doing so, it will show up in the Stage Manager instead of the dock
7. You may resize your app window to fill the screen by dragging its boundaries, rather than by hitting the green button, if you wish it to.
8. Point your cursor to the far left of the screen to view the other application in Stage Manager. Now that the thumbnails have appeared, you may continue to use Stage Manager as normal.

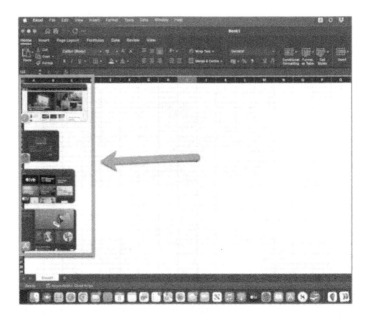

9. A thumbnail that you previously scaled to fill the screen will return at this exact size when you click on it.

How to Use Several Apps and Groups in Stage Manager

Stage Manager may also be used to group applications together so they launch simultaneously or to manage numerous windows of the same application.

Using Stage Manager with several applications:

1. Numerous windows of the same application, such as numerous Word documents, will show up in the same thumbnail when you open them

2. By default, when you click this thumbnail, Stage Manager will remain open while each window opens one at a time. As shown in the next section, it is possible to modify this behavior such that clicking the thumbnail opens each window for that application individually.

3. You may make a group of windows that will function similarly to a single thumbnail if you wish to utilize many apps at once. This group of windows will be associated with the same application.

4. To do this, launch the app you want in your group first, followed by the second. The Stage Manager will receive the first app.

5. Select this thumbnail with a click, then drag it into the main window next to your second app.

As an alternative, you can click the thumbnail while holding down Shift

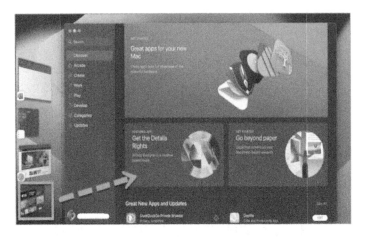

6. Now both applications will take the front stage. You can resize or rearrange them, but you shouldn't place them in Split Screen mode because doing so would take them out of Stage Manager.
7. Your new group will show up as a single thumbnail when you launch another app or group from Stage Manager.

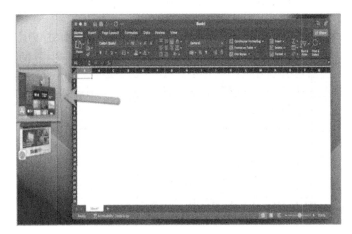

8. Both applications will launch in the identical locations that you previously configured when you click on this thumbnail
9. You may drag an application to the left in the Stage Manager to remove it from a group, or you can click the app window while holding down Shift.
10. Drag files or folders over the relevant thumbnail until it moves to center stage to shift them from a center stage app to one that is in the Stage Manager sidebar. After that, you may drop the files normally
11. To prevent some applications from showing up in Stage Manager, use Cmd+H when the app is in the center of the stage. In Stage Manager, the application window will be hidden and invisible. Click the app's Dock icon to launch it again.

How to modify Mac Stage Manager Settings

There aren't many options in Stage Manager for Mac, but the ones that you do have may have a big impact.

To modify the Stage Manager's settings:

1. To access the System Settings, click the Apple symbol.

2. Scroll down to the Desktop & Dock option on the left and click it.

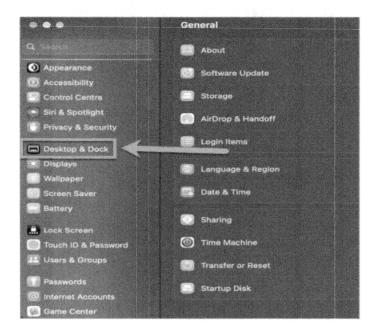

3. Select the Stage Manager toggle switch and then click the Customise option under Windows & Apps.

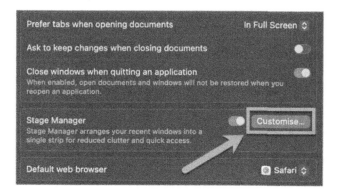

4. Recent Applications arranges the apps you've used most recently on the side of the screen. They won't show up if you disable this until you move your cursor to the far left of the screen

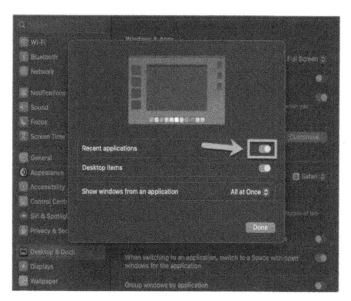

5. Desktop Items control whether Stage Manager is open and displays the files and folders on your desktop.

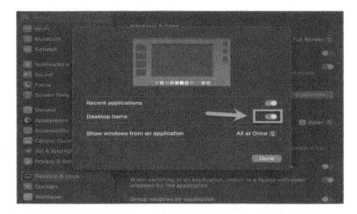

6. Displayed Windows modifies the behavior of an application when working with numerous windows for the same program can be altered
7. All At Once: Clicking the app's thumbnail causes all windows to launch simultaneously.
8. Clicking the thumbnail of One At A Time opens a single window.

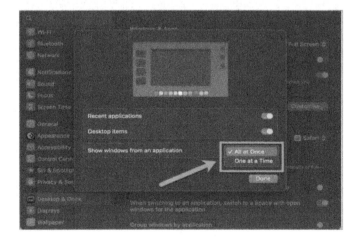

CHAPTER 10

How to move data from your Old to your recently purchased Macbook Air

Your data and preferences may be moved to your new Macbook Air from an existing Mac or PC.

Before starting

- Update the operating system on both your new and old computers to the most recent version

- Ensure that both computers are linked to the same network to transfer data wirelessly.

Moving or transferring files from one Macbook to a different one

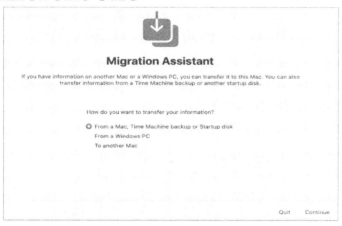

Migration Assistant

If you have information on another Mac or a Windows PC, you can transfer it to this Mac. You can also transfer information from a Time Machine backup or another startup disk.

How do you want to transfer your information?

○ From a Mac, Time Machine backup or Startup disk
From a Windows PC
To another Mac

Quit   Continue

Utilize Migration Assist.

- You may now move files via the old Macbook to the new one with Migration Assistant. Files via your old Macbook are copied by Migration Assistant; they are not erased.

With your latest Mac

1. On your brand-new Mac, launch Migration Assistant. It's located in your Applications folder's Utilities folder. Next, select "Continue."

2. Input your administrator passphrase when Migration Assistant requests authorization to make changes, then click OK.

3. Choose the option to move via a Macbook, or Time Machine backing-up, up or begin loading the disc when prompted about how you wish to move your data. Next, select "Continue."

Via your old Mac

1. Take your old Macbook and open Migration Assistant. It's located in your Applications folder's Utilities folder. Next, select "Continue."

2. Choose to move your data to another Mac when prompted about how you would like to transfer it. Next, select "Continue."

Via Time Machine backup

Via your latest Mac

1. Choose the other Mac when prompted to choose a startup disc, Time Machine backing-

up, or additional device. Next, select
"Continue."

Transfer information to this Mac

Select a Mac, Time Machine backup, or other startup disk to transfer its information to this Mac.

MacBook Pro

Other Server...

Looking for other sources...

Make sure that the other Mac, Time Capsule, or disk that you are transferring from is connected
to the same network or directly connected to this Mac.

When transferring from another Mac, open the Migration Assistant app in the Utilities folder on
that Mac and select "To another Mac".

Current Wireless Network: Wi-Fi   Change...

Back   Continue

Via your latest Mac

Verify if the security code you see matches the one
displayed on your new Macbook. Next, select
"Continue."

Using your latest Macbook Air

1. Migration Assistant measures the amount of
    storage space utilized by your programs, user
    accounts, docs, folders, & preferences in
    addition to cataloging all of the stuff on your
    previous Mac. This may need many minutes.
    When you're ready, choose which data to send

2. Understand what happens when you move a
    user account before selecting Continue.
    Migration Assistant requests to replace or

rename an account if it already exists on the new Macbook with the same name:

- Rename: With a different sign-in & home file on your new Macbook, the account from your previous Mac will show up as an extra user.

- Reinstate: The account on your previous Mac will take the place of the account with the same name on your current Mac.

3. Large transfers may take hours to finish and may appear to halt periodically. Perhaps you might begin in the nightfall and let the migration finish overnight. To commence the move, hit on Continue

4. To see the files from the transferred account on your latest Macbook, log in to Migration Assistant when it has finished on both machines.

Transfer information to this Mac

Select a Mac, Time Machine backup, or other startup disk to transfer its information to this Mac.

MacBook Pro

Other Server...

Looking for other sources...

Make sure that the other Mac, Time Capsule, or disk that you are transferring from is connected to the same network or directly connected to this Mac.

When transferring from another Mac, open the Migration Assistant app in the Utilities folder on that Mac and select "To another Mac".

Current Wireless Network: Wi-Fi   Change...

Back   Continue

How to Activate AirDrop

Sharing files or links between your Mac and other Apple devices is made easier with AirDrop. All Apple devices typically have AirDrop enabled by default, but if you have an older Mac or have already turned it off, here's how to activate it again.

Keep in mind that you can also activate AirDrop on a more recent MacBook Air by selecting Control Centre from the menu bar and then selecting AirDrop.

1. Launch the Mac's Finder app
2. hit on Go

3. Select AirDrop
4. Select the person you want to find out about your Mac from the list at the bottom of the window.

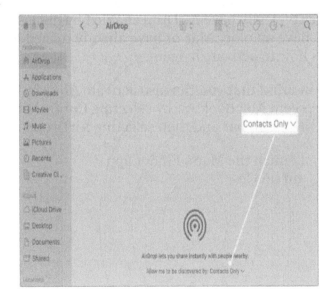

5. AirDrop is now available for file sharing and receiving.

Sending a Folder via AirDrop

It's simple to transfer a file with AirDrop once it's enabled on your Mac and other devices.

Note: When sending a file to your iPhone, it will open in the Files app, but a photo will go straight to your Photos app. Links will launch in the browser of your choice.

1. Locate the file on your Mac first
2. Select "Share."

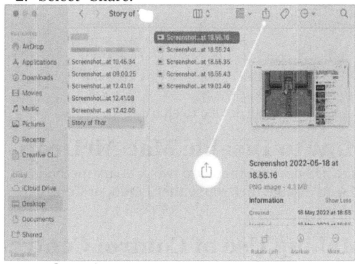

3. Select AirDrop

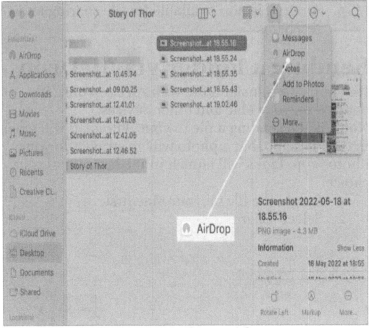

4. Select the device to share with.

How to Disable Mac AirDrop

Like iOS devices, there are two primary methods on a Mac to disable AirDrop: either Finder or Control Centre.

Making Use of Control Centre

1. To launch Control Centre, click the icon located in the upper-right corner of the menu bar.
2. Select AirDrop

3. To disable AirDrop, click the toggle (the blue to grey symbol will change).

88

How to Use the Finder

1. Launch the Finder.
2. From the sidebar, choose AirDrop

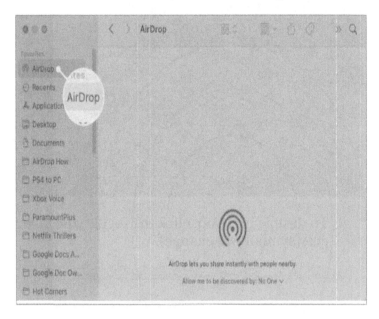

3. Choose No One from the Allow Me to be Discovered by dropdown menu.

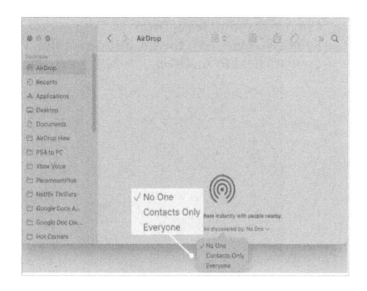

You can also use the technique below a try.

1. Go into System Preferences
2. Choose General.

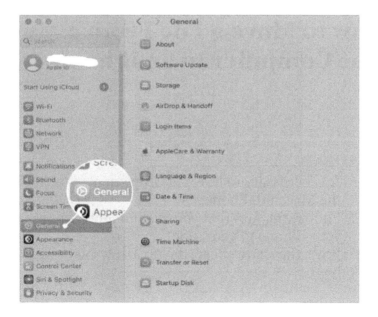

3. Choose Handoff & AirDrop.
4. Select No One from the drop-down option that appears next to AirDrop.

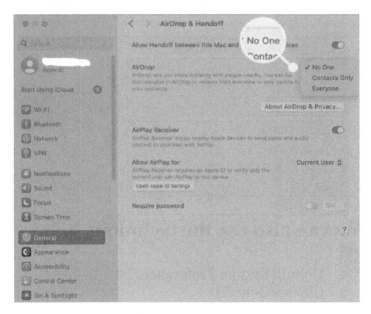

How to Move a File From a Mac Computer to an iPhone

Share or move folders via iPhone to your MacBook Air utilizing AirDrop

1. It is necessary to have AirDrop enabled on both the Mac and iPhone.
2. Choose the files that you wish to move from your iPhone to your Mac.
3. Press the share sheet (the up arrow-pointing box).

4. The first choice in the first row can be your Mac. In such a case, press it to send the file. Then select AirDrop.
5. To transfer the file, tap the Mac icon.

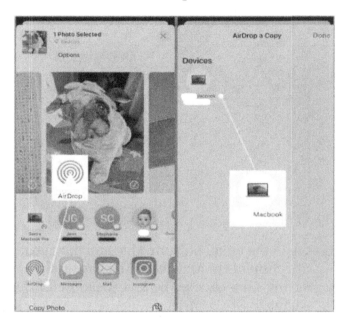

How to Move Files from iPhone to Mac Using Email

Email has been useful for distributing information for as long as we have been able to attach files to them.

1. Choose the file (here, it's a photo, but it works with any app that allows sending files)
2. Give the share sheet a tap.
3. Select Mail.
4. Enter your email address in the To: area (make sure this email is configured on your Mac)
5. Press the transmit button

6. Open the email on your Mac and download the attachment (in Mail, click the paper clip > saving All > choose the Mac location for the file saving).

How to Sync Data Between an iPhone and a Mac

Note: Not every app allows for this type of file transfer, so you can't move every file on your iPhone in this manner.

1. Use USB to connect your iPhone to your Mac (Wi-Fi connections are also an option).
2. Launch a new window in the Finder (on Windows, open iTunes, and move on to step 4).

New Finder Window

3. Click your iPhone in the Locations area of the sidebar (you may need to click Locations to enlarge it).

4. Select Files

5. This displays iPhone apps that are capable of transferring files to your Mac. To view the files for each program, click the down arrow.
6. Drag and drag the desired file to your desktop or another location on your hard drive.

Use iCloud Photos to Transfer Images from iPhone to Mac

1. Toggle the iCloud Photos slider to the on/green position on the iPhone by navigating to Settings > Photos.

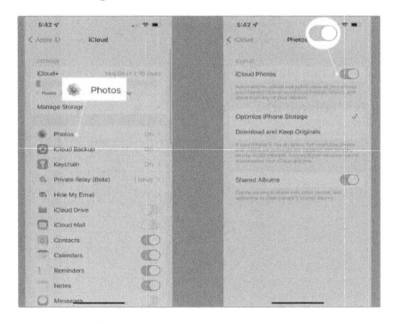

2. Launch the Photos app on the Mac, then select Photos > Preferences.

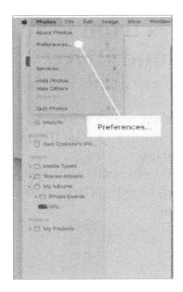

3. Select the iCloud Photos check box.; all images and videos on your iPhone will now be automatically transferred to iCloud Photos. The image or video will be ready for you the next time you open the Photos app on your Mac.

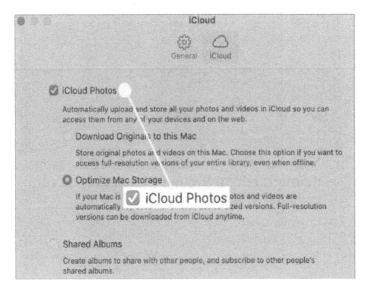

Move Files from iPhone to Mac Using iCloud Drive

File sharing between devices is a breeze using Apple's iCloud.

1. You must sync with iCloud Drive to transfer files over iCloud. On the iPhone, select Settings to get started

2. Press and hold [your name] > iCloud > iCloud Drive > change the On/Green slider for Sync this iPhone

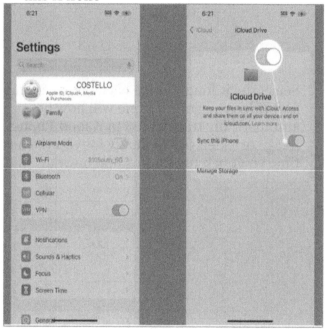

3. Next, turn on your Mac to sync in the same manner. Hit on System Preference via your gadget's Apple menu

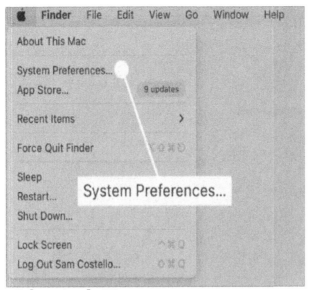

4. Select Apple ID

5. Select iCloud
6. Select the iCloud Drive checkbox

7. Launch a fresh Finder window and enlarge the sidebar's iCloud area.

8. Select iCloud Drive. Everything that your iPhone synchronized is here. To finish the download to your Mac, click the download icon.

Chapter 11

Setup Messages for Mac

Setup iMessage

1. Input your Apple ID & passphrase in the Messages program on your Mac, then select Sign In

2. Select SMS > Settings, then hit on iMessage, Settings, and choose one of the settings listed below:

Stop using iMessage

You may log out of iMessage if you would like to stop seeing text on your Macbook.

1. Choose text > Settings, select iMessage, and then click Settings from within the Messages program on your Mac

2. After clicking Sign Out, make sure you intend to signing-out. You end up getting text on your Macbook when you sign out of iMessage.

Message someone on a Mac

1. To begin a new message in the Messages program on your Macbook, hit on the Compose knob (or utilized the Touch Bar)

2. Enter the recipient's designation, mail info, or handset number in the To section of the message. Messages propose addresses as you

write, either from contacts in the Contacts application or via individuals you've messaged before

3. Type your message into the window's bottom area. If accessible, you can use the typing suggestions

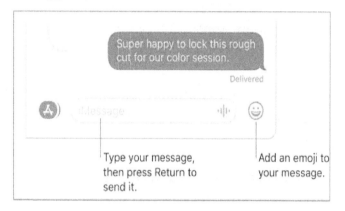

Type your message, then press Return to send it.

Add an emoji to your message.

4. To send the message, click the Send button or hit Return on your keyboard.

Texting or sending text to groups

1. To begin a new message in the Messages program on your Macbook, click the Compose button (or use the Touch Bar)

2. Enter each person's name, phone number, or email address in the To section of the message form. Messages propose addresses as you write, either from contacts in your Contacts app or from individuals you've messaged before. In addition, you have the option to click the Add button to the right of the to area. After

selecting a contact from the list, click the phone number or email address.

3. Type your message into the window's bottom area. If accessible, you can use the typing suggestions.

Use Business Chat to send a text to a company

1. On your Mac, use Maps to find the company you wish to speak with or launch a mail via the company

2. Click a link in the email or the Message button on the Map Info page to initiate a conversation. If this is your first communication with this company, a fresh dialogue will start. If not, you are free to carry on with your discussion.

3. Type your message into the window's bottom area, then hit Return. The types of content that you may add are the same as those that you will be sending text to groups or individuals.

Un-send or modify a message on Mac

Undoing a sent text or SMS

A recently sent message can be resent up to two minutes after it was delivered.

1. Select a discussion from the Messages program on your Macbook

2. Choose Undo Send by controlling-clicking the text or attachment.

Adjust a sent text or SMS

Within fifteen minutes of sending a message, you can change it five times.

1. Choose a conversation containing the text you intend to change in the Mac Messages program

2. To edit the message, control-click it and select Edit (or use Command-E)

3. Adjust as necessary, then hit Return.

Utilize Tap-back in a text via your Macbook

You may quickly and easily react to messages with a **LIKE** or **DISLIKE** fingers using tap-backs.

1. Choose a discussion from the Messages program on your Mac

2. Take one of these actions:

- To send a tapback, select a tapback by clicking and holding a message. You may as well hit or tap a text and then hit a Tapback via the Touch Bar if your Macbook has one.

- To remove a tapback, select the same tapback that you sent by clicking and holding the message. You may as well hit on a text & then hit the same Tapback on the Touch Bar if your Macbook has one.

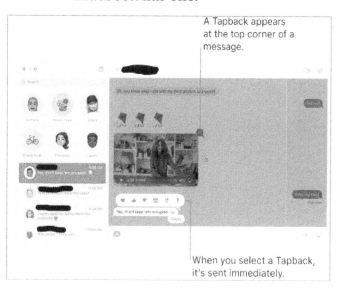

A Tapback appears at the top corner of a message.

When you select a Tapback, it's sent immediately.

Sending an audio message via your Macbook

- Select a discussion in the Mac version of the Messages program, now hit on the Record Audio icon to record a text

- Touch the Stop knob to halt recording

- Hit on the Play knob (button) to read the message before sending it

- Click the email button or hit Return on your keyboard to email it.

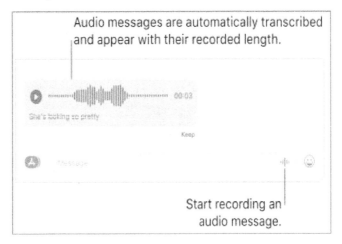

Audio messages are automatically transcribed and appear with their recorded length.

Start recording an audio message.

Personalize the messages

Modify the Mac's Messages settings.

1. Select Messages > Settings from inside the text application on your Macbook, then select an option from the menu via the upper section of the window:

Make your Memoji on Mac Messages

You may make a customized Memoji that expresses your personality using macOS 11 or later. Next, send a Memoji to let your messages reflect how you're feeling.

1. Pick any discussion from the Messages program on your Macbook

2. Hit on the Memoji button after clicking the Stickers button and Apps buttons leftward via the text box

3. To build and personalize your Memoji, click the Add or More buttons, depending on whether it's your first one. Then, follow the on-screen directions to change anything from the skin tone to the clothes

4. Select "Done."

Blocking text in messages on your Macbook

Block or ban texts from a certain individual or phone number.

1. Choose a discussion from the Messages program on your Macbook

2. Choose Conversation > Block individual from the menu bar, then click Block.

Control unwanted calls

1. Select Messages > Settings, select iMessage, and then click Blocked in the Messages application on your Macbook

2. Take one of these actions:

    - To block a contact, hit on the Add knob and choose the desired contact name from the list

    - To delete a banned contact, first, choose the desired name or number from the blocked caller's list, now hit on the Remove knob.

Creating & controlling contacts in Mac Messages

Messages are where you may generate & manage your contacts.

Creating a fresh contact

If the individual you are messaging is not in your Contacts, you may add them by creating a contact card.

1. Choose a discussion from the Messages program on your Macbook

2. Hit on Conversation > Add or include to Contacts from the menu bar

3. Complete the contact card's fields. Make sure you input the credentials for any instant

messaging services you wish to use to communicate with the individual.

You may either input the new contact's name in the Messages window's To box or select them from a list by clicking the Add button adjacent to the To field.

Modify a person's name to look differently in the sidebar

When you're messaging someone, you may open their contact card from the chat and add their name, so that you see that on the sidebar instead of just their phone number or email address.

1. Double-click a discussion in the sidebar of the Mac Messages program to open it in a separate window.

Click the Search bar in the top-left corner and type your search terms to find contacts and material in chats. Alternately, pick from the suggested images, links, contacts, and more.

2. Place the pointer above the mail or handset number in the To search bar, then select Add to Contacts by using the down arrow

3. In the window's lower-left corner, select Contacts

4. Take any of the popped-up actions:

Chapter 12

Customize your display

Your Mac's System Preferences

1. Start by clicking the System Settings logo via the Dock or selecting Apple icon menu > System Setup, then

2. Touch the preferred setting via the side or flank-bar.

Choose the color scheme for your Mac.

Click an item in the sidebar to adjust settings.

Lock the screen

After a certain amount of inactivity, you may configure your Macbook Air to either turn off the display or launch a screen saver. If you need to access the screen on your Mac again, you may also need to enter a password.

- Navigate to Lock Screen under System Settings to configure.

Select a screen protector

While you use slow-motion screen savers as your wallpaper or while you're not using your Macbook Air, the display might become an artistic creation.

1. Navigate to Screen Saver under System Settings to configure.

2. By selecting "Show as wallpaper," you may set any of the screen savers—Landscape, Cityscape, Underwater, Earth, or Shuffle Aerials—as your background.

Remember your forgotten passwords

Passwords that you keep in iCloud Keychain or on your Mac may be seen in System Settings. After selecting Passwords from the sidebar, log in to your Macbook Air.

- Click the information icon for the website you want to view your password for, then

- Move your cursor over the password to see it.

- Moreover, you may click the information icon to share it using AirDrop or update or remove it as a password.

Sharing passphrase & passkeys with others

To examine the passphrases & lock keys you wish to share, create a group of trusted contacts. Your passkeys and passwords remain current even if you make modifications.

1. Slide to System Preferences & hit on Passphrase. After selecting a New Shared Group and giving the group a name,

2. Touch the Add knob & choose Add People.

3. Click Add once you've entered the names of the recipients you wish to share with.

4. Choose the group,

5. Hit on the Add knob (button),

6. Pick Move Passphrases to a Group,

7. Pick the accounts you intend to share, & then

8. Click Move to share passwords with the group.

Personalize the menu bar and Control Centre.

1. Select the options you wish to show up in your menu bar or Control Centre.

2. Select Control Centre from the sidebar of System Settings after making your selection.

Update macOS.

To check if your Mac is running the most recent version of macOS software,

1. Select General from System Settings and then

2. Click Software Update.

Family Sharing and iCloud configurations

Using your MacBook Air,

1. Log in to iCloud via your Apple ID

2. Control how your apps utilize iCloud, and configure and oversee Family Sharing.

Utilizing System Setups to personalize your Macbook

You may personalize your Mac by adjusting the system settings. You may select a bright or dark appearance, alter the background, and do a lot more.

1. Either select the Apple icon menu > System Settings or hit on the System Setups Settings logo via the Dock

2. Select an option.

    - On your Mac and the installed programs, the settings are shown in the side or flank bar & may change.

3. Modify a selection.

Open System Preference on your Macbook to locate options.

To personalize your Macbook via words & phrases you know, navigate to the system settings. Optional parameters are also available for selection.

Search field   Options that match your search

A setting with options
that match your search

Locate a setting option in the System Settings

1. Either select Apple icon menu > System Settings or hit on the System Setups logo via the Dock

2. Type a term or combination into the search bar

3. Under the find bar field are settings that include selections that match the content of your search

4. Touch or pick an item via the given list.

Select a recommended setting

1. Either select the Apple icon menu > System Setups or hit on the System Setups (settings) logo via the Dock

2. Press the search button.

   - Based on the settings you use most frequently, suggestions are made.

3. Choose or hit on an option via the given list.

Return to the Mac system settings that you previously viewed

You may go through any system configuration you have lately viewed. A list of the system settings you have recently viewed is another option.

Navigate through the settings you were most recently in

- Either select the Apple icon menu > System Setups or hit on the System Setups (Settings) logo via the Dock

- Examine the settings as you usually would.

- To return to the settings you were just in, click the Back or Forward buttons at the top of the window.

Every time you enter System Settings, your history of recent settings is refreshed.

Select a setting from a list of previously seen options

1. Either select the Apple icon menu > System Setups or hit on the System Setups (Settings) logo via the Dock

2. Examine the settings as you usually would.

3. To choose a setting, slide the pointer over it and then release it after pressing and holding the Back or Forward buttons at the top of the window.

Every time you enter System Settings, your history of recent settings is refreshed.

Adjust your system screen display language

1. Select System Preferences from the Apple menu on your Mac (the subsequent alternative in the menu), now choose & hit General on the side or flank bar and Language & province via the right.

2. Select one of the following actions under the catalog of chosen languages at the top:

    • Include a language: hit on the Add knob (the button via the lower-rightward angle), choose a language via the list, and then click Add

    • Modify the main language: Move your preferred language to the front of the list of languages.

Choosing your preferred language for every application

1. Select System Preferences from the Apple menu on your Mac, then select General on the side or flank bar &Language & province on the right.

2. Select Applications and take one of the following actions:

    • App language selection is as simple as clicking the Add button, selecting the desired app and language from the pop-up options, and then clicking Add.

- Modify an application's language from the list: After selecting the app, a pop-up menu will appear; select a new language.

- Take an application off the list: After choosing the app, press the Remove option. Once more, the program speaks in its default tongue.

Make your screen text & other icons bigger

To make everything on the screen larger, you may adjust the display resolution. You can also enlarge text and icons to make them easier to view.

Increasing display size & icons

You will be able to enlarge the displayed icons, logos, widgets, and the hoist of others on the screen by adjusting the resolution of your monitor.

1. Select System Preferences from the Apple menu on your Mac, then select Displays via the side or flank bar.

2. Touch on the gadget's resolution rightward.

All the elements on the screen are larger when the resolution is decreased.

Enlarge text and icons in all applications and system components

To change the preferred text reading size in different programs, on your gadget desktop, & in side or flank bars, all you need is one slider.

1. Select System Preferences from the Apple menu on your Mac, then select Accessibility via or in the side or flank bar.

2. Select "Text size" after clicking on Display via the rightward section, now select Text.

3. To increase the font size or extent on the desktop, via or in the side or flank bars, & via the listed applications (if they are configured to Utilize ideal Reading range (size), move the slider rightward.

Enlarge text for certain applications or system components

You may change the text's reading size within a lot of programs. Desktop sidebars and labels both have text size adjustments available.

-   Within applications: You may use the **Command** (+) or **Command** (−) keys to modify the font size when reading mails, texts, & editorials in Mail, and reports, among other apps.

- Additionally, you may utilize System Preferences to designate a preferred text reading size for certain apps, such as Messages, Calendar, and Mail. See the section above on system features including making text and icons larger across applications.

- On webpages: To change the text size in Safari, use Command-Option-Plus (+) or Command-Option-Minus (−).

- In the Finder's file and folder names: Select View > Display View Parameters. Select a text size by clicking the "Text size" pop-up menu.

Note: In Gallery view, font size cannot be altered. Refer to Modify the Finder's folder display settings.

- Desktop labeling: Select the "Text size" pop-up menu by Control-clicking the desktop, then select Show View Options.

- Sidebars: Select System Preferences from the Apple menu, then click Appearance (you will have to navigate or slide downward). Select Large from the pop-up option that appears next to "Sidebar icon size" on the right.

Change the resolution of your Mac display

The size of text and objects on your screen will be based on the resolution of your display.

Adjust the resolution on your main monitor.

1. Select System Preferences via the Apple icon menu on your Mac, then select Displays in the sidebar.

2. Pick on a resolution.

   - If the available resolutions are displayed in thumbnail form, drag the cursor above the thumbnails to examine the sizes of the resolutions, then select the desired one by clicking on it.

   - Control-tap on the thumbnail outlook & select Show List to display the various resolutions as a catalog. After that, pick the desired resolution.

   - Control-tap the catalog outlook & select Show Thumbnails to return to the thumbnail view.

Adjust the linked display's resolution.

More options for resolution become available if you have more than one monitor after it is connected.

1. Select System Preferences from the Apple menu on your Mac, then select Displays in the sidebar.

2. After choosing the display to modify, choose the resolution you wish to employ.

It could be possible for you to view more display resolutions if you enable "Show all resolutions."

CHAPTER 12

Split Screen

Utilize your Mac Split Screen

How to Use Mac Split Screen in macOS Sonoma

Although the split screen has been there since macOS Catalina, the setup process was somewhat altered in that version and hasn't changed since.

The instructions in the following section must be followed if you're running an earlier version of macOS.

When using macOS Sonoma to split screen:

1. Select the window you wish to use for split screen
2. Hover your cursor over the window or click and hold the green full-screen button for it.

3. Via the list that appears, pick Tile Window to Leftward of Screen or Tile Window to Right of Screen.

4. That side of the screen will see the window shift. Choose a different window from the ones that are displayed on the other side of the screen.

5. Split screen mode will now be enabled for your two windows.

Utilize Mission Control to Utilize Split-Screen on your gadget

via your Mac, you may also utilize Mission Control to split-screen two windows. Depending on the kind of computer you are using, there are a few different ways to access Mission Control.

Utilize Mission Control to split-screen via your new gadget:

1. Decide which window to utilize in split-screen mode
2. To enable full-screen mode for the window, click the green full-screen icon
3. To activate Mission Control on your Mac, use the F3 key. Another option is to hit Ctrl+Up
4. You may also use three fingers to swipe up if you're using a laptop. Apply two fingers to the double-tap if you're using a Magic Mouse
5. The window that you set to full screen will be shown on the screen's top bar.
6. Choose which other window to make full screen. You may move it up onto the window you wish to match it with by clicking and holding it.
7. To pick the split screen window, click on it.
8. The two windows will now be shown side by side in split-screen mode.

How to Use a Mac in Split Screen Mode

You can work in both windows once you're in split-screen mode. While operating in split screen mode, there are a few key points to remember.

1. To work in a window, click anywhere in it.
2. To access the menu for the window that is now open, move the mouse to the top of the screen
3. Click the other window's menu to view it, then drag your mouse to the top of the screen
4. Click and drag the bar that separates the two windows to adjust their sizes

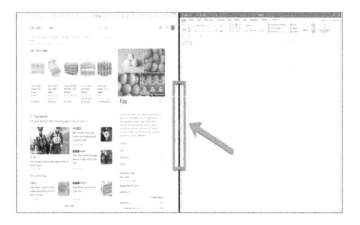

5. Click the bar at the top of a window and drag it to the opposite side to switch sides. The other window will slide into the vacant place on its own
6. You may swipe left or right with three fingers on your Mac trackpad to go to other applications, or you can hit F3 to launch Mission Control.

7. Click and hold the green full-screen button in either window when you're done with split screen mode, then choose Exit Full Screen.

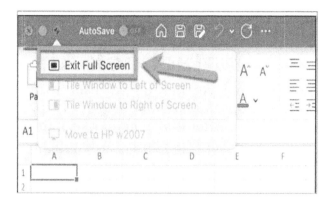

CHAPTER 13

Taking a Screenshot on your Macbook Air

Using a screenshot, you may quickly capture the windows and icons that are now displayed on your Mac or PC screen. After that, you may keep the picture for your records or share it with others.

Taking screenshots is simple for Macbook Air users because of the built-in features, which let you quickly generate and store personalized screenshot photos. You may use this detailed tutorial to learn how to snap a screenshot on a Mac.

Taking a Mac Screenshot via Complete Screen

Using a keyboard command is the quickest way to snap a full-screen screenshot on a Mac.

- Via your keyboard, press Shift + Command +3.

After saving, you may use the desktop to see or modify this image.

Custom Area Screenshot

- Use the keyboard shortcut Shift + Command + 4 to do this. The region you wish to take a screenshot of may be chosen using the new mouse cursor.
- To take a screenshot, pick the area you wish to capture with your mouse or trackpad. The snapshot will be saved to your desktop in the customary location when you release the mouse.

Screenshot via menu bar pop-up

- Via your keyboard shortcut, hit **Shift + Command + 5**. On some MacBooks, it will also show up if you click the screenshot icon in the touch bar.
- After activating the pop-up, you'll be presented with several options to customize the screenshot's appearance. They consist of the capacity to take a screenshot of the full screen, a window that is displayed, or to pick a region with your mouse or trackpad.
- To accomplish this, pick an option from the bar and then drag or tap the corresponding screenshot. To capture a visible window, for example, choose the Capture Selected Window option and use your mouse to pick the window.
- This section can also be used to record your screen activities for later usage. These recordings are stored on your desktop like

movies, however, screen captures created in this manner will not include internal audio.

- To abort your snapshot or screen capture, click the cancel (X) button located on the menu bar's left side.

How to Modify the Mac's Screenshot Save Location

- To start, load the bar by hitting on the Shift + Command + 5. Choose Options when the bar at the bottom of your screen displays.
- To store your screenshots, pick another pre-specified place (like Documents) at the top, or click Other places to enter your location. If you select Other Location, a pop-up Finder window will appear where you may select a new folder for your screenshots.

Crop a Mac Screenshot

These include techniques that let you use filters to enhance your photo, crop off undesired exterior parts, or make more sophisticated adjustments. Here's what to do on a Mac if you want to crop a screenshot.

Making Use of the Integrated Screenshot Cropping Tool

The easiest way to crop a screenshot on a Mac may be to use the recently included built-in tool.

On the lower-right corner of your screen, a floating thumbnail will appear as soon as you take a screenshot on macOS. It's a screenshot thumbnail that, when clicked, opens the cropping tool. You won't be able to utilize the tool if you don't click on the thumbnail within a few seconds. Regrettably, there is no way to prolong the period before it disappears.

Utilizing this tool to crop:

- Once your screenshot has been taken, click the Crop icon (top-right)
- Hit on the section of your screenshot you would prefer to store
- Click Done once you're done.

Utilizing Preview

The Preview application launches automatically on macOS when you double-click a picture. This application allows you to easily crop screenshots.

With Preview, crop a screenshot as follows:

- In Finder, double-click a picture to launch the Preview application.
- Click the Show Markup Toolbar icon (pencil-shaped symbol, top-right).
- To pick the region you want to keep, click and drag it.
- Tap Tools from the menu bar.
- Hit on Crop via the televised menu.

Utilize Photos application to crop

On macOS, the built-in tool for organizing your photo collection is the Photos app. Moreover, you may use it as a simple picture editing application on a Mac, which lets you easily crop screenshots.

To edit screenshots with the Photos app:

- Navigate to Photos and select File > Import.
- Choose the screenshot that you wish to modify
- Click Import.
- After double-clicking the imported picture, select Edit (top-right)
- Hit on the Crop knob or button via the upper section.

CHAPTER 14

Personalize your Mac's wallpaper image

The image that appears on your desktop can be changed. Use your photographs or pick from a range of Apple's given images or colors.

1. Select System Preferences from the Apple menu on your Mac, then select Wallpaper in the sidebar.

2. Choose a background image from among the accessible groups:

3. Customize your wallpaper's settings.

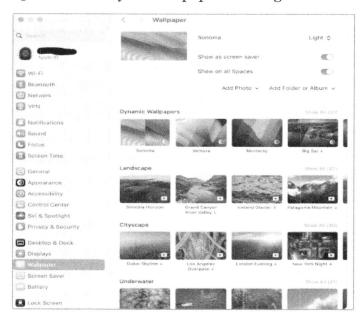

Mac wallpaper settings

- To alter the image or color displayed on your Mac's desktop (the portion of the screen that serves as the screen's backdrop), go to the Wallpaper settings

- See the specifics about adjusting your settings by looking through the choices below

- Select the Apple menu > System Preferences, then select Wallpaper from the sidebar to access these changes.

Include a picture

- Pick a photo to utilize as your wallpaper. The images you've selected appear via the lower section of the window, beneath Your Photos

- From the pop-up menu next to the current wallpaper thumbnail, select how you want the picture to cover the screen

- To navigate between the pictures, use the Rotate button located beneath Your Photos. Pick randomly to modify the order & pick the duration every photo via the televised list adjacent to the recent wallpaper thumbnail will be shown.

Add an album or folder

Include a selection of pictures for your wallpaper. Pictures from the selected album or folder appear at the window's bottom.

- Via the onscreen directives menu shown after the thumbnail of the live wallpaper,

- Pick how you intend the image to show on your gadget display

- To rotate amid the images, hit on the Rotate knob positioned underneath the file or catalogs designation.

- Select Randomly to change up the order and

- Choose how long each picture via the televised menu adjacent to the existing wallpaper thumbnail will be displayed.

Dynamic or Lively Wallpapers

Select a photo to utilize as your gadget's wallpaper.

1. Select an appearance via the televised menu that appears next to the thumbnail of the active wallpaper:

   - Automatic: Depending on your present position, it automatically changes via brightness to dim at sunset

- Dynamic: Changes color gradually depending on the day duration where you are

- Brightness (Still): The desktop shows a low-resolution, static copy of the image.

- Dim (Still): The desktop shows a black-and-white, still image of the image.

2. When a Dynamic or lively Wallpaper designation has a downward arrow after it, it indicates that the picture must be downloaded. To download the picture, click it.

Rotate Aerials

You may set your background to alternate between many aerial photos.

- Select the frequency of aerial rotation from the pop-up menu located next to Shuffle at the top of the window

- Whenever you're not utilizing your Macbook, toggle on "display as screen saver" to utilize slow-mo aerials so to hide the desktop.

Photos
- Choose & hit on a photo to utilize as your wallpaper.

- An image that has a down arrow next to it indicates that it needs to be downloaded

- Touch the photo to install it.

Colors

- Select a hue for your wall covering

- in favor of your background, hit on the Rotate knob to cycle via the variety of hue or color

- To include a color, click the Add button.

Pictures, Records, and Folders

- Select your wallpaper from the albums, folders, and pictures you've uploaded.

Choose between a bright and dark theme for your Macbook

Via your Macbook, you may choose between a bright and dark appearance for the menu bar, Dock, windows, and built-in programs.

1. Select System Preferences from the Apple menu on your Mac, now hit Appearance in the side or flank bar.

2. On the right, choose brightness, dim, or Auto.

Modify Mac Night Shift settings

To adjust these parameters, select System Preferences from the Apple menu, then hit Display via the side or flank bar, and finally hit the Night Shift icon on the right.

Setting up the Night Shift

After confirming that your Mac satisfies Night Shift's system requirements, take these actions:

1. Select System Setups (or System Favorite) from the Apple menu

2. Select Shows

3. Toggle the Night Shift on

Here, you may design your own Night Shift schedule, configure it to activate automatically from dusk until dawn, or manually switch Night Shift on and off until dawn or the designated time. When the Night Shift is on, you may also adjust the color temperature to be somewhat warmer.

Schedule

- Select the option to enable Night Shift on its own at specific times

- Observe the Shift to a tepid hue on your Mac at sunset and a certain period during the night.

Turn on warmer hues on your Mac at a certain hour of the night

1. Select System Preferences from the Apple menu on your Mac, then select Displays in the sidebar.

2. Select Custom from the pop-up menu that appears after clicking the Night Shift icon on the right

3. Select the start and finish times for the Night Shift, then click Done.

Switch to warmer colors on your Mac around sunset.

Step 1: **Setup the time zone and activate Location Services**

You have to activate Location Services to utilize this option.

1. Select System Preferences from the Apple menu on your Mac, then click Privacy and Security from the sidebar.

2. Toggle on Location Services by clicking the Location Services button on the right

3. Select Details after swiping down to reveal System Services

4. Hit on Done once you have toggled on **Setting the time zone**

Step 2: **Enable Night Shift, which runs from dawn to dusk.**

1. Select System Preferences via the Apple icon menu on your Mac, then select Displays in the sidebar.

2. Hit sundown to daybreak from the Schedule pop-up menu by clicking the Night Shift icon on the right.

   - Activate it till tomorrow.

   - Pending the subsequent day, or pending when you toggle it off, leave the Night Shift on.

Adjust the color (hue) of your Macbook manually to warmer hues

1. Select System Preferences via the Apple icon menu on your Mac, then select Displays via the side or flank bar.

   - Select the "Turn on until [time]" option after clicking the Night Shift knob via the rightward angle.

2. Pending when you toggle it off or pending the subsequent day, the Night Shift is activated.

Color (hue) temperature

Night Shift employs a color temperature that may be changed.

On your Mac, adjust the color temperature of your display.

1. Select System Preferences from the Apple menu on your Mac, then select Displays in the sidebar.

2. To adjust the color temperature that Night Shift employs, click the Night Shift icon on the right and move the slider.

CHAPTER 15

Widget

Adding and customizing widgets for Mac

To monitor your schedule, favorite gadgets, weather, top stories, and more on your Macbook, include widgets to the display or notice Centre.

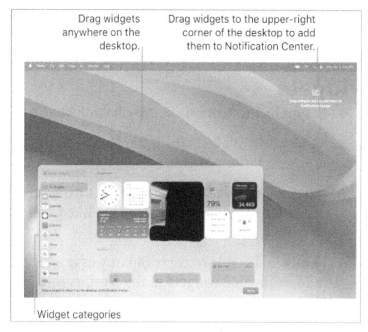

Drag widgets anywhere on the desktop.

Drag widgets to the upper-right corner of the desktop to add them to Notification Center.

Widget categories

1. Hit on the date & duration in the menu icon or use two fingers to slide left via the rightward angle of the trackpad to launch Notification Centre. Click anywhere on the desktop to end it.

Add or include widgets to your display desktop

1. On your Macbook, choose Edit Widgets by Control-clicking the wallpaper

2. Look for a widget using the widget browser. Alternatively, choose a category—like Clock—to see the widgets that fall under it

3. Utilize any of the subsequent techniques to include widgets to the display desktop:

4. Hit on Done via the widget browser's lower-right corner when you're done adding widgets.

Adding Notification Centre widgets

1. Launch Notification Centre on your Mac.

2. Select Edit Widgets from the Notification Center's bottom menu.

3. Look for a widget using the widget browser. Alternatively, choose a category—like Clock—to see the widgets that fall under it.

4. You will be able to carry out any of it after that, add or include widgets to the Notification Centre:

5. Hit on Done via the widget browser's lower-right corner when you're done adding widgets.

Utilize Mac widgets for iPhones

1. Select System Preferences from the Apple menu on your Mac, then select Desktop & Dock via the side or flank bar.

2. Select Widgets and activate "Use iPhone widgets."

Personalize widgets

1. Control-click a widget on your Mac

2. Take any of these actions:

3. Click Done when you're done modifying the widgets.

Take the Notification Center's widgets down.

1. Launch Notification Centre on your Mac

2. Take one of these actions:

3. To get rid of a widget, control-click on it and select Remove Widget from the shortcut menu.

4. Point the cursor over the widget you wish to delete, now hit on the Remove knob (button) while holding down the Option key.

Modify the widget's settings.

1. Select System Preferences from the Apple menu on your Mac, then select Desktop & Dock via the side or flank bar.

2. Select Widgets located on the right

3. The checkboxes adjacent to "Show Widgets:" can be selected or deselected

4. Select an option from the "Widget style" pop-up menu by clicking on it

5. Activate or deactivate "Use iPhone widgets."

Utilize a Mac screen saver

When you need more privacy or whenever you're not utilizing your Mac, you may use a screen saver to hide the desktop.

Personalize the Mac's screen saver.

1. Select System Preferences from the Apple menu on your Mac, then select Screen Saver from the sidebar.

2. Choose a screen saver via the several categories that are offered:

3. Configure your screen saver.

CHAPTER 16

MUSIC

Find songs

Use the Mac's Music app to find music.

Search Apple songs

1. Click the search box via the top-leftward angle of the Mac's Music program

2. On the right, click Apple Music.

3. Write or input your search word (i.e. a music theme or lyric), then click Return or choose from the suggested results.

Find your music collection.

1. Click the search box in the top-leftward angle of the Mac's Music program

2. On the right, select Your Library

3. Insert or input your find terms (i.e., artist or album name), choose an option, or hit Return.

Check for songs via the iTunes

1. Click the search box in the top-leftward angle of the Mac's Music program

2. On the right, select iTunes Store.

- Select Music > Settings, click General, confirm that iTunes Store is chosen, and then click OK if it isn't shown there.

3. Type in your search term (for example, a song's lyrics or genre of music), choose an option, or hit Return.

Select music from your preferred genres.

1. Click the search box in the upper-left corner of the Mac's Music program.

2. Decide on a style, tone, or pastime, like dancing or fitness.

Find tracks in Music on Mac by using the column browser

1. On your Mac, choose Songs from the sidebar of the Music program

2. Select the columns you wish to have shown by selecting View > Column Browser > Show Column Browser.

   - The columns' order cannot be altered.

3. Choose selections from one or more columns in the column browser.

Song selections that fit your criteria are shown below as you make your selections.

Discover music in Mac Music via the filters

1. Click any item beneath Library or any playlist in the sidebar of the Mac's Music program

2. Enter the criteria you wish to match by clicking the Show Filter Field button in the top-right corner.

Items that fit the criteria stay as you enter them. Click the Cancel button to return to the full list of songs.

Use Mac Music to play music from your collection.

1. To locate songs in your music collection using the Mac's songs program, try any of the following:

   • Locate a certain song or album: Select any item from the sidebar below Library. For instance, select Albums to see every album in your library.

   • Select a playlist. From the sidebar, select a playlist by clicking on it

   • Examine your music collection: See Music Search.

2. Click the Play button after moving the pointer over any song or album.

Streaming suggested music from Apple Music

1. Use the Mac's Music program to search for music you wish to play by doing any of the following:

    - View personalized recommendations: Find music you've recently played, custom playlists made just for you, genres you might enjoy, and more by clicking the Listen Now button on the sidebar.

    - View Apple Music's latest additions: Discover music by mood, new releases, charts, and more by clicking the Browse button on the sidebar.

    - Locate custom playlists: To view playlists tailored to your listening preferences and past selections, select Made For You from the sidebar.

    - Check for the Apple song library:

2. Hover your cursor over any song, playlist, or album, and then press the Play button.

Play the Apple Music radio in Mac Music

Playing a station

- Select Radio from the sidebar of Apple Music in the Mac Music app.

- Click the Play button after moving the pointer over any station, program, or playlist.

Set up a station

Any of the locations (below Library in the sidebar) where you may play a song, such as Playlists or Albums, can have a station created for you.

1. Click any option in the sidebar below Library in the Mac's Music program. Click Songs, for instance, to see every song in your library.

2. After selecting an item, select Create Station from the More menu.

Click Listen Now or Radio in the sidebar (below Recently Played) to access the new station.

Play music together on a Mac with SharePlay

SharePlay may be used to listen to music together.

1. To begin playing music on your Mac during a FaceTime chat, move your pointer over any song or album in the Music app and click the Play button

2. All callers can perform the following while listening together:

- Manage the playback (switch to the next song, pause the music, and more): Use the Touch Bar or the buttons on the playback controls.

- Control the shared Playing Next queue: You may change the order or remove music, add songs, albums, and playlists, and do a lot more.

- See the lyrics: Check out the lyrics using the Full-Screen Player.

3. Click the SharePlay symbol in the menu bar and then the Close button in the upper-right corner to end the FaceTime connection.

Create SharePlay to launch automatically

You can configure SharePlay to launch automatically whenever you use it if you don't want it to the first time.

- Click the SharePlay icon in the menu bar, click the SharePlay button on the right, and choose Automatically under SharePlay for Music while you're listening to music.

Use Mac Music to listen to an online broadcast

1. Select File > Open Stream URL from the Mac Music app

2. Type in the whole URL of the file or broadcast that you wish to listen to.

Change the volume of the Music

1. You can play music from your CD collection, stream music from Apple Music, play Apple Music radio, or listen to web broadcasts using the Mac's Music program

2. Select one of the following actions to regulate the volume:

   o Adjust the level for every song (just like you would on a stereo): Utilize the Music window's volume slider, located near the top.

   o Volume-adjust a certain song or music video: Click Options, choose Song > Info, and then drag the volume slider.

   o Make sure that the loudness of all songs and music videos is always the same: Click Playback under Music > Settings, then choose Sound Check.

3. Click the AirPlay button and choose the checkbox next to the speaker to utilize speakers other than the built-in ones.

Personalize your listening experience

Shuffle or replay tracks via your music

1. Play music from your CD collection, stream music via Apple Music, or use the Music app on your Mac.

2. Take any of these actions:

   o Activate shuffle: From the playback controls, select the Shuffle button

   o Mix and match albums or groups: Select Albums (or Groupings) under Controls > Shuffle

   o To shuffle the tracks in an album, hover your cursor over any album in your collection, and select Shuffle [album name] from the More menu.

   o Play every song in the view that is now open (like a playlist): Select "Repeat" from the menu. When the button changes color, repeat is activated.

   o Repeat the song that is now playing: Press the Repeat button until you see the number 1

   o Disable repeat: Till the button turns grey, click the Repeat button.

Put your music in order in Music on Mac

Utilize the queue

1. Play music from your CD collection, stream music via Apple Music, or use the Music app on your Mac

2. To play a song and the ones that come after, double-click it after selecting the Playing Next option

3. To end the queue, click the Playing Next button once again.

Utilize Autoplay

1. Play music from your CD collection, stream music via Apple Music, or use the Music app on your Mac

2. To enable Autoplay, click the Playing Next button, Playing Next, and finally the Autoplay button at the top of the queue.

The button's color changes when Autoplay is enabled. To toggle it off, hit on it again.

Organize and add songs to the queue

1. Browse through your collection or Apple Music in the Mac Music app. Then, select the More button (it looks like this or this), and hit on any of the subsequent actions:

- Play Next will move the song to the front of the queue

- Include some music at the back of the queue: Select "Play Later."

2. Select Playing Next by clicking the button, and then take one of the following actions:

   - Drag the tracks into the desired order to adjust the queue's music order

   - Take a tune out of the queue: After choosing the music, hit the Delete key.

   - Take every song out of the queue: In the queue, select the Clear link.

View the music you've played lately

- Click the Playing Next button in the Mac Music app, then

- Select History.

Arrange tracks in Mac Music.

To play your songs in a certain sequence, sort them using the Sort pop-up menu or, for a faster sorting option, by clicking on the column headers

Sort using the pop-up menu

To rearrange the song, album, or playlist order in your music collection, use the Sort pop-up menu located anywhere on the page. You have the option to display all of your music or just your top selections.

1. Click any item beneath Library or any playlist in the sidebar of the Mac's Music program

2. Select any of the following actions after clicking the Sort pop-up menu in the upper-right corner:

   o Select the tracks to be sorted: Select whether to sort all of the [items] or only the ones you have favored.

   o Select the order of sorts: After selecting a sort order (such as Time and Ascending), click Sort Options

   o Include extra columns for sorting: Select which more columns to display by clicking Show View Options

3. To start the music playing in the order you've selected, double-click the song you wish to play first.

Sorting via clicking the column headers

To easily sort the songs in your music collection, click on one of the column headings in the song list.

1. Click Songs in the sidebar of the Mac Music program, located beneath the Library

2. To play music in alphabetical order by album, artist, or song title, click the heading of any column (or sort by any other category).

  o Select View > Show View Options to display other categories.

3. To start playing music, double-click on it. Depending on the sequence you choose, the remaining songs play after that.

Find the Music files

1. On your Mac, choose Songs from the sidebar of the Music program

2. Take one of these actions:

  o Find the location of a file: After selecting the item, select Song > Info.

  o The File pane's bottom (next to the location) displays the file's path.

  o Open the file in the File Manager: Once the item has been selected, select File > Show in Finder.

  o The file could be in your music library rather than on your machine if you are unable to access Show in Finder.

Modify the import files' storage location

1. Select Music > Settings from within the Mac's Music program, and then select Files

2. Select a new place for your files by clicking Change.

Organize your files into a single Music folder.

1. Select File > Library > Organize Library from the Mac Music app

2. Choose "Combine files."

Copies are stored in the default folder, but original files are kept in their original places.

Convert audio file types in Mac Music

1. Select Music > Settings from within the Mac's Music program, and then select Files

2. Select Import Preferences.

3. Within Import Select the format you wish to convert music to using the pop-up menu, then click OK to preserve the changes

4. Pick one or more tracks from your music collection, then select File > Convert > Generate [format] Version.

Adjust the music settings

- Select Music > Settings from within the Mac's Music app, and then click any of the following options that pop up

Chapter 17

Family and friends

Setup your Macbook Family Sharing

1. Select System Preferences from the Apple menu on your Mac, then select [your name] in the sidebar's upper section.

    - If your name is not displayed, choose "Sign in with your Apple ID," type in your password, your Apple ID, and any Reachable At email addresses or phone numbers you may have selected in the Apple ID settings. You will be able to create or generate an Apple ID if not having any yet

2. Select Family Sharing from the menu on the right, then select Set Up Family before sending out invitations to family members:

    - Invite your family along: After selecting Invite People, adhere to the on-screen directions.

    - Create a younger child's Apple ID: Then adhere to the on-screen steps after selecting Create Child Account.

3. Click Add Member, then adhere to the on-screen directions to include more family members in your Family Sharing group.

4. Take any of the popped-up actions:

Configure a child's screen time on a Mac

Using family sharing to set up and monitor a child's screen time is the most adaptable and practical method. Using Family Sharing on any Mac, you can remotely control and keep an eye on each child's device usage from your account.

1. Perform one of these actions on your Mac:
   - If family sharing is being used, then: Make sure you are logged in with your Apple ID after logging into your Mac user account
   - Enter the child's Mac user account to log in if you are not using Family Sharing.
2. Select System Preferences from the Apple menu, then select Screen Time from the sidebar.
3. Select a child by clicking the pop-up menu on the right if Family Sharing is enabled
4. Select Set up Screen Time for Your Child, select Turn on Screen Time, and then adhere to the prompts displayed on the screen.
   - You may establish time away from displays, set content limitations, enable Screen Distance, enable App & Website Activity, and generate a 4-digit Screen Time passcode during the setup process.
5. Scroll down to the Screen Time settings and enable any of the following:
   - Include Website Data: Select this option to enable the inclusion of particular website visitation information in Screen

Time reports. In the absence of this setting, webpages are simply recorded as Safari uses.

- Lock Screen Time Settings: Select this option to lock Screen Time settings and grant more time when limitations are reached.

Set Screen Time on Mac to impose privacy and content limitations

1. Perform one of these actions on your Mac:
   - Make sure you are logged in with your Apple ID when you log into your Mac

user account if you are using Family Sharing.

- Enter into the Mac user account of a family member if you are not utilizing Family Sharing.

2. Select System Preferences from the Apple menu, then select Screen Time from the sidebar.

3. Select a family member by clicking the Family Member pop-up menu on the right if you're a parent or guardian in a Family Sharing group

4. If it isn't turned on already, click Content & Privacy and turn it on

5. Click material Restrictions and toggle the settings on and off to limit access to web material

6. Click Store Restrictions, then toggle the settings on or off to limit the purchase of movies, TV series, and apps

7. Click App Restrictions and toggle the settings on and off to restrict apps

8. Click Preference Restrictions, then toggle choices on or off to lock certain settings.

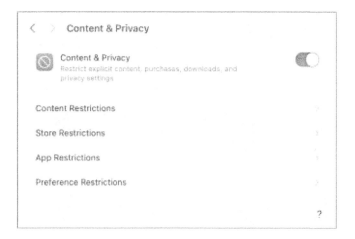

Utilize Screen Time on Mac to schedule downtime

You and your kids can make a timetable for when you and they spend time together away from screens. Moreover, downtime may be turned on or off as required, saving you from having to adjust the timetable.

Create a downtime schedule.

1. Perform one of these actions on your Mac:
   - Make sure you are logged in with your Apple ID when you log into your Mac user account if you are using Family Sharing
   - Enter into the Mac user account of a family member if you are not utilizing Family Sharing.
2. Select System Preferences from the Apple menu, then select Screen Time from the sidebar.
3. Click the Family Member pop-up menu on the right, choose a family member, and then click Downtime if you're a parent or guardian in a Family Sharing group.

167

- You must enable Screen Time for the chosen family member if you are unable to see Downtime.
4. Select an action from the Schedule pop-up menu by clicking on it
   - Set a daily routine for your downtime: After selecting Every Day, type the start and finish timings
   - Decide on a distinct nap time for every day of the week: After selecting Custom, input the start and finish hours for each day and toggle downtime on or off.
5. Select Block at Downtime if you wish to block the device during that period.

You can only use this option if you have a Screen Time passcode.

Activate or deactivate the downtime schedule

1. Perform one of these actions on your Mac:
   - Make sure you are logged in with your Apple ID when you log into your Mac user account if you are using Family Sharing.
   - Enter into the Mac user account of a family member if you are not utilizing Family Sharing.
2. Select System Preferences from the Apple menu, then select Screen Time from the sidebar.

3. Select a family member by clicking the Family Member pop-up menu on the right if you're a parent or guardian in a Family Sharing group
4. Select Downtime, then choose an action from the Schedule pop-up menu:
   - Activate the downtime schedule by selecting Custom or Every Day
   - To disable the downtime schedule, choose Off.

Immediately turn downtime on or off.

1. Perform one of these actions on your Mac:
   - Make sure you are logged in with your Apple ID when you log into your Mac user account if you are using Family Sharing
   - Enter into the Mac user account of a family member if you are not utilizing Family Sharing.
2. Select System Preferences from the Apple menu, then select Screen Time from the sidebar.
3. Select a family member by clicking the Family Member pop-up menu on the right if you're a parent or guardian in a Family Sharing group.
4. Toggle Downtime on or off by clicking on it.

A youngster is alerted that downtime starts in five minutes when you enable it for them.

Configure Communication Safety in Mac Screen Time.

1. Try any of the subsequent on a Macbook:
    - Enter your Apple ID after logging into your Mac user account
    - Open a child's Mac user account and use their Apple ID to log in.
2. Select System Preferences from the Apple menu, then select Screen Time from the sidebar.
3. Select a family member by clicking the Family Member pop-up menu on the right if you're a parent or guardian in a Family Sharing group
4. Select Safety of Communication
    - Toggle the **Check for Sensitive Picture** function on/off.
    - The Screen Time passcode might need to be entered.

< > Communication Limits

 Communication Limits
Limits apply to Phone, FaceTime, Messages, and iCloud contacts.
Communication to known emergency numbers identified by Will's carrier is
always allowed.

During Screen Time

Allow communication with
Allow one-on-one and group conversations only with people in Will's contacts.

Everyone
○ Contacts only
Contacts and groups with at least one contact

During Downtime

Allow communication with
During downtime, allow one-on-one and group conversations only with specific
people in Will's contacts.

Contacts Only
○ Specific contacts   Select Contacts...

Manage Will's iCloud Contacts:

?

CHAPTER 18

Facetime on your Macbook Air

Use a Mac to make and receive FaceTime video calls.

Making a video call via Facetime

FaceTime video calls allow users to view and converse with one another.

1. Click New FaceTime in the FaceTime application on your Mac to initiate a FaceTime video call
2. Type the recipient's phone number or email address into the New FaceTime box. You might have to hit Return.
3. Either utilize the Touch Bar or click FaceTime.

Answering or Taking a FaceTime video call

When a notice shows in the upper-right corner of the screen on your Mac; hit on any of the subsequent actions:

- **Answer a call that comes in**: Press the Accept icon shown on the screen
- **To accept a video call as an audio call**, select Answer as Audio by clicking the down arrow next to Accept. The camera turns off

172

automatically when you're on a phone call or audio call.

- Click End & Accept to accept a call and end the one you are currently on.
- Select "Decline" to end a call.

Turn down a FaceTime video chat

When a notice shows in the upper-right corner of the screen on your Mac, choose one of the following actions:

- Select Decline to end a call.
  The person calling will notice that you're not at the office.
- Utilize iMessage to refuse a call & send a text: hit on the downward arrow logo after the reject logo or icon, hit on the Reply via text icon, input your write-up or text, and now hit on the Send icon. The caller and you both need to be logged into iMessage
- Turn down a call and make a note to return the call later: To set the time for when you wish to get a reminder, click the down arrow next to Decline. When the time arrives, a notification appears on your screen. Click it to see the reminder, then click the link to initiate the call.

Stop or Close a FaceTime video chat
- Place the cursor over the call window, then
- Select the Leave Call button (cancel red icon) or (use the Touch Bar) to stop the call.

Use your Macbook to make & receive group FaceTime calls

Launch a fresh FaceTime group chat

1. Select New FaceTime from the FaceTime app on your Mac
2. Enter each person's phone number or email address to add them to the New FaceTime window by adding them as callers. You might have to hit Return.

You may choose to choose the individual from Suggested or input their name if they are saved in your Contacts.

3. Click FaceTime to initiate the Group FaceTime call, or use the Touch Bar or the down arrow to choose FaceTime Audio.

Include extra participants in a FaceTime video chat

1. Click the Sidebar button in the menu bar when on a FaceTime or Group FaceTime video conference on your Mac, and then select Add People.
2. Type a contact's name, phone number, or email address into Contacts. (You might have to hit Return.) Additionally, you can choose a person from Suggested.
   In the to area, provide the contact details for each person you want to add at once.
3. Select Add.

Note: Click the Sidebar button and then select Ring to send an alarm to a caller who hasn't joined the call yet.

The screen displays each participant's picture or initials as a tile. The tile of the person on the call advances to the front and becomes more noticeable when they speak or when you click on it.

Adding additional participants to an audio FaceTime call

- Click the microphone button in the menu bar when on a FaceTime or Group FaceTime audio chat on your Mac
- After selecting the Add People button, input each person's phone number or email address that you wish to contact. You might have to hit Return.
  You may just type in the person's name or choose them from Suggested if they are already registered in your Contacts.
- Select Add.
  Note: Click the Sidebar button and then select Ring to send an alarm to a caller who hasn't joined the call yet.
  The screen displays each participant's picture or initials as a tile. A circle encircles the speaker's picture or initials as they talk.

Answering or Taking a FaceTime group call

- On your Macbook, **choose Join**, and then on the FaceTime box, **select the Join** Video button.
- A group FaceTime call may also be accepted via Messages. **Click Join** in the FaceTime **messaging box** when you are invited.

Reject a FaceTime group video call

When a notice shows in the upper-right corner of the screen on your Mac, choose one of the following actions:

- Click Decline to end a call.

Pausing or muting a group FaceTime video call

During a FaceTime or Group FaceTime session, your camera is momentarily disabled when you pause the video. Talking on the phone, everyone can still hear each other.

- Click the **Mute Video logo** on your gadget's screen in the FaceTime app.
- **Note: The camera remains on when you click the yellow "minimize" button at the top of the FaceTime window, but the video may halt. In the Dock, click the FaceTime icon to switch on your camera again.**

Joining a FaceTime call on your Mac via a link

- Click the link to the FaceTime call, then select Join in your Mac's FaceTime software.

The call starts if you are the one who created the FaceTime connection. Those who created the FaceTime link can join the call right away. Participants using Apple devices have the option to admit new callers once they have been on the call for 30 seconds.

CHAPTER 19

Privacy and security

Use Your Screen Time

Screen Time allows you to keep an eye on your kids' computer usage and restrict their access to websites.

1. Hit on System Preference via the Apple logo menu, now

2. Select Screen Time from the sidebar.

Make use of Safari's privacy features.

Safari offers a plethora of capabilities to assist you in managing your online privacy.

Browse secretly using Mac Safari.

When you surf in private, neither the websites you view nor the data of your browsing activity are shared with your other Apple devices.

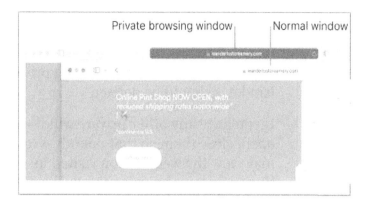

Private browsing window   Normal window

Browse once secretly

1. Select File > New Private Window from the Safari software on your Mac, or open an existing private browsing window

2. Proceed with your usual browsing.

Always surf in privacy

1. Open the Safari software on your Mac, select Preferences > Safari > General

2. Select "A new private window" from the "Safari opens with" pop-up option after clicking it.

Select Apple menu > System Settings, click Desktop & Dock in the sidebar, and then enable the option labeled "Close windows when quitting an application" on the right if you aren't able to see it.

Quit using private browsing.

1. To open a non-private window in the Safari software on your Mac, select File > New Window, exit the private window, or go to a non-private window

2. Utilize any of the subsequent proceedings to develop privacy for others:

- Anything you downloaded using private windows should be deleted

- If you have any other private windows open, close them so that nobody else may view the website you visited in those windows by using the Back or Forward buttons.

Clear your browser history.

1. Select History > Clear History from the Safari app on your Mac, then click the pop-up menu.

2. Select the extent to which you wish to delete your internet history.

Utilize Mail Privacy Protection

You may enable Protect Mail Activity in Mail settings if you didn't when you initially opened Mail.

1. Select Mail > Settings from within the Mac Mail program, and then select Privacy

2. Choose Mail Activity Protection.

Adjust Mail's privacy settings on a Mac

1. Select Mail > Settings, then Privacy in the Mail program on your Mac to modify these settings.

Block or unblock senders on your mail

Blocking senders

1. Choose a message from the sender you wish to ban in the Mac Mail program

2. In the message header, move the pointer over their name, click the arrow, and select Block Contact.

Unblocking blocked senders.

1. Choose a message from the sender you wish to unblock in the Mac Mail program

2. In the message header, move the cursor over their name, click the arrow, and select Unblock Contact.

Use Mail on a Mac to Hide My Email

Send an email with a special, arbitrary address.

Hide My Email gives you the option to generate a special, random address right within the Mail app when you compose a new email message.

1. To start a new message in the Mail software on your Mac, click the New Message icon

2. Fill up the recipient and message topic fields.

- Sending messages from a distinct, random address can only reach one recipient.

3. Hover your cursor across the From box.

4. Select Hide My Email from the pop-up option that displays.

5. After writing your message, select Send when you're ready.

Restrict whoever has access to your Macbook camera

You can shoot pictures and videos with your Mac's camera by installing certain programs. Which applications are permitted to utilize the camera is up to you.

1. Select System Preferences from the Apple menu, then select Privacy & Security in the sidebar.

2. Select the correct camera icon.

Update to macOS Mojave or later if you are unable to view the Camera.

Log in to your Mac using Apple Sign

Using Apple Sign-in to access applications and websites is a simple and private method. It makes it easier to sign in every time by using your Apple ID to safely create an account with an app or website. You don't need to fill out a form, validate your email address, or pick a new password.

Create an account from an application or a web page

1. If an app or website asks you to register for an account, click the sign-in button or, if it's not accessible, select Continue with Apple on your Mac

2. conform with the instructions on your display screen.

Log in to your account from an internet site or application

1. Click the button to log in or proceed with Apple on your Mac.

2. If your Mac or Magic Keyboard supports Touch ID, use it. If not, enter your login password on your Mac (you might also need to enter your Apple ID password).

Modify the Apple settings for a website or app's sign-in

1. Select System Preferences from the Apple menu on your Mac, then click [your name] in the sidebar's upper section. Click Sign in with Your Apple ID if your name isn't displayed to enter or create one

2. Next to Applications Using Apple ID, click Edit after selecting Sign-In & Security on the right

3. Select a website or app from the sidebar, then take one of the onscreen actions:

Configure your Mac to be safe.

Here are some steps you may take to increase the security of your Mac.

1. Make use of strong passwords

   - Use passwords to encrypt your Mac to protect your data, and make sure the passwords are difficult to figure out

2. Create or generate a passphrase

3. Make users log in

4. Keep your Mac safe when it's not in use

5. After your Mac wakes up, ask for a password

6. Keep the number of administrative users to a minimum.

Configure your Mac to log out when not in use.

1. Select System Preferences from the Apple menu on your Mac, then pick Privacy & Security from the sidebar.

2. Select Advance from the bottom menu.

3. Select "Automatically log out after inactivity."

4. Select the duration of time before the user is automatically logged out by clicking the "Log out after" pop-up menu.

Safeguard your data
do this by

1. Making frequent backups

2. limit permitted access to your Info

3. Immediately install software updates

4. Steer clear of dangerous software

Creating a pass key

Use a passkey to access an account on your Mac.

Using a passkey eliminates the need to generate and remember a password to access an app or website account. A passkey employs Touch ID or Face ID to verify your identity in instead of a password.

first of all, Configure iCloud Keychain on a Mac so that data automatically fills in.

Set up iCloud Keychain.

1. Hit on System Preference via the Apple logo menu on your Macbook, now

2. Select [your name] in the sidebar's upper section.

   • Click "Sign in with your Apple ID" if your name is not displayed, then enter your password after entering your Apple ID (or a Reachable At email address or phone number that you provided in Apple ID settings). If you lack an Apple ID, you can generate one.

3. Toggle on Sync this Mac by clicking iCloud on the right, then Passwords & Keychain

4. If you haven't already, follow the on-screen directions to set up two-factor authentication.

Apple ID two-factor authentication

To ensure that you are the only one with access to your account, two-factor authentication is in place. Find out how two-factor authentication functions and how to enable it.

To ensure that you are the only one who can access your account—even if someone else knows your password—two-factor authentication adds an extra degree of protection to your Apple ID.

For the majority of Apple IDs, two-factor authentication is the default security mechanism.

Activate two-factor verification on your Apple ID

Using a Mac:

1. Select System Preferences from the Apple menu by clicking on your name.
2. Select Security & Sign-In
3. Click Turn On next to Two-Factor Authentication and
4. Hold on and trail the directives on the display screen.
   - Online: Visit appleid.apple.com and enter your Apple ID to log in. After providing your security question answers, click Proceed. When prompted to improve account security, tap Proceed. Next, choose Upgrade Account Security and adhere to the prompts displayed on the screen.

186

Utilize two-factor authentication to log in and obtain a verification code.

To sign in with your Apple ID on a new device or browser, you will require a verification number if you are using two-factor authentication.

Using a Mac

1. Select System Preferences from the Apple menu by clicking on your name
2. Select Two-Factor Authentication under Sign-In & Security
3. Press the Verification Code button.

CHAPTER 20

Using find MY

Configure Find My on a Mac

On your Mac, you may enable Find My to help you find it and secure it if it is lost or stolen. Along with finding your Apple products and gadgets, you can also share your position with others.

Activate the location services.

- To enable Find My to locate you, turn on Location Services
- Select System Preferences from the Apple menu on your Mac, then select Privacy & Security from the sidebar.
- On the right, click Location Services.
- Activate Location Services, and then select Find My from the app list.

Activate Find My Mac.

To find, lock, or erase your Mac info, enable Find My Mac in the iCloud settings.

1. Select System Preferences from the Apple menu on your Mac, then select [your name] in the sidebar's upper section. Click "Sign in with

your Apple ID" to log in or create an Apple ID if you can't see your name

2. Select Find My Mac after selecting iCloud on the right. (Click Show All if Find My Mac isn't listed.)
   - Activate Location Services first if there is a caution badge on the Find My icon.
3. Select Turn On, and when prompted to allow Find My Mac to utilize your Mac's location, select Allow
4. You can choose to enable or disable the Find My Network.
   - Hundreds of millions of Apple devices are connected to the encrypted, anonymous Find My network, which can assist you in finding your device even while it is offline.
5. Select "Done."

Find a device on a Mac by using Find My

You may use the Mac's Find My app to track down a lost Apple device and receive alerts when it is found. You must add a missing gadget to Find My before it becomes missing to find it.

See the location of a gadget

1. Click Devices in the Mac's Find My app
2. Choose the device you wish to find from the Devices list
3. If the device can be found, its location is shown on the map. The device's name is displayed below the updated location and timestamp.

If the device cannot be discovered, the message "No location found" is shown beneath the device's name.

If a device's last location was submitted to Apple more than seven days ago, the device's position might not be located.

Search for a gadget location

1. Select Devices from the Find My program on your Mac.
2. Choose the device you wish to receive instructions for from the Devices list, then click the Info button to view the map
3. Toggle on Directions

Receiving an alert once a gadget is found

1. Select Devices from the Find My program on your Mac
2. Choose the device you wish to receive notifications for from the Devices list
3. On the map, click the Info button, and then toggle the Notify When Found setting.

Use iCloud.com's Find Devices feature to find a device.

- Go to icloud.com/find to log in to Find Devices.

Find your gadget

- Choose the device from the All Devices list on the left when using iCloud.com's Find Devices feature

- Click All Devices to go back to the list and choose a different device to find.

Mark a gadget as lost on Mac.

1. Select Devices from the Find My program on your Mac
2. Click the Info button on the map after selecting the device you wish to label as lost from the Devices list
3. Select Activate next to Mark As Lost
4. Pay attention to the directions displayed on the screen
5. For a Mac, click Activate or Lock.

Verify the whereabouts of a reported missing device

1. Select Devices from the Find My program on your Mac
2. Click the Info button on the map after selecting the device you wish to verify from the Devices list
3. One of the following status remarks shows underneath the Mark As Lost section when a device is designated as lost:
   - When you label a device as lost when it's not connected to Wi-Fi or a cellular network, Pending will show up until the device reconnects.
   - Activated: The item is reported missing as soon as it connects to the internet.

Modify the missing device's message

1. Select Devices from the Find My program on your Mac.
2. Click the Info button on the map after selecting the device you identified as lost from the Devices list.
3. Select Pending or Activated under Mark As Lost
4. Click Done after updating the message or phone number.

Toggle between AirTag and other items in Find My on Mac's Lost Mode

You may safeguard your personal information by using Lost Mode in the Find My app on your Mac if you are unable to locate your AirTag or third-party item

How is an item protected by Lost Mode?

An item's Lost Mode allows you to write a message indicating that it's lost and providing contact information. If someone else discovers your item, they can see a webpage with the message on a device that is compatible.

Activate Lost Mode

1. Click Items in the Mac's Find My app

2. Click the Info button on the map after selecting the object you want to indicate as lost from the Items list
3. Click Enable next to Lost Mode.
4. As directed by the on-screen guidance. Choose "Activate."

Modify the phone number displayed in the Lost Mode alert.

1. Click Items in the Mac's Find My app
2. Click the Info button on the map after selecting the item you identified as lost from the Items list
3. On the Enabled menu, select Lost Mode.
4. Once the phone number has been changed, click Done.

Disable your AirTags or any item's Lost Mode in Find My on Mac

1. Click Items in the Mac's Find My app
2. Click the Info button on the map after selecting the item you identified as lost from the Items list
3. On the Enabled menu, select Lost Mode
4. To confirm, click Turn Off after selecting Turn Off Lost Mode.

Disable Mark as Lost in Mac Find My

You may disable Lost Mode in the Find My app on your Mac, or unlock a Mac by entering the password or passcode, once you've located the device you reported missing.

View item details on a Mac in Find My

1. Click Items in the Mac's Find My app.
2. Choose the thing you wish additional information about from the Items list, click the Info button on the map, and then scroll to the bottom.

Personalize find MY

Modify the appearance of the map in Mac Find My

You may zoom in or out, alter the map view, and examine the map in three dimensions.

View your present location.

1. Select your current location by clicking the button in the map's lower-left corner.

Look at a 3D map

In the map's lower-left corner, click the 3D button. To change the angle, use the slider in the lower-right corner. Before things display in 3D on the map, you might need to enlarge them.

CHAPTER 21

Printing documents via your Macbook printer

1. Select File > Print or hit Command-P when your Mac is open and a document is selected.

   - When the Print dialogue box opens, a preview of your printed document shows.

2. Click Print to finish if all the options in the Print dialogue are correct.

3. Select any of the following typical print settings to modify the printing options:

Select a paper size for your printed document on Mac

You can establish a default paper size for regular printing and select a paper size that corresponds to the sheet size of your printer.

Modifying the size (dimension) of the printing paper

The paper size that you use in your printer may be customized.

1. Select File > Print when your Mac is open and a document open

2. Select a paper size from the pop-up Paper Size option.

Modify the default paper size that you usually print on.

1. Select System Preferences from the Apple menu on your Mac, then click Printers & Scanners from the sidebar.

2. From the "Default paper size" pop-up menu on the right, select a paper size.

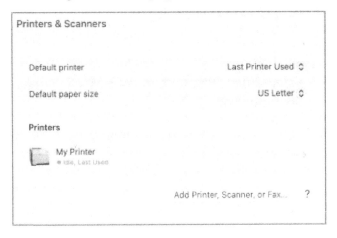

CHAPTER 22

Troubleshooting common problems

How to Fix a Mac That Doesn't Power Off

Applications can occasionally become unresponsive and interfere with the Mac OS's ability to shut down correctly. This is how to stop non-responsive applications via force.

1. Choose Force Quit from the Apple menu by clicking on it in the top left corner of the screen. Alternatively, you may use the keyboard shortcut Command + Option + Esc to access this menu

2. Locate a program with Not Responding next to it in the Force Quit Applications window.

3. Select the name of the unresponsive program and select Force Quit. Try shutting down the Mac again after forcing the program to exit

4. To switch off the Mac, hold down the power button for a brief period if forcing a quit doesn't resolve the issue. Sadly, any unsaved work is lost if you have to take this course.

Backing up your Macbook

You will be able to utilize Time Machine to routinely back up your stuff, including docs, mail, song, pictures, applications, & more if you have an exterior storage gadget like a USB drive.

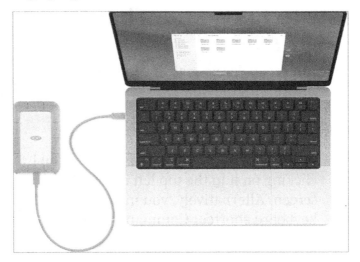

Pair a storage device with a Macbook

Link an exterior storage device, i.e. as a USB/thunderbolt drive

Connecting the Drive

1. Plug the hard drive into the Macbook via the cord that came with it.

2. verify your drive via your desktop

3. launch the drive to see its items & files. Double-tap the drive on your system display screen or choose it via the left frame of a Finder window to view the contents of the drive

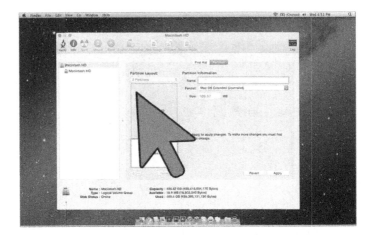

Formatting a New Drive

1. First, launch the Disc Utility

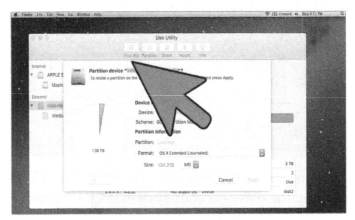

2. From the option on the left, choose the hard drive

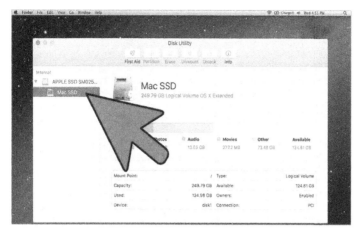

3. In the Disc Utility box, click the "Erase" button at the top. The drive formatting procedure will begin as a result

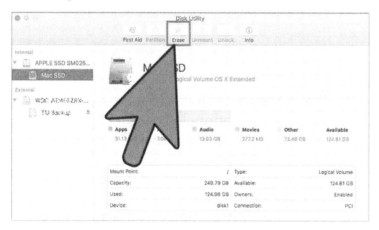

4. Hit on the "Format" tab & hit on "ExFAT"

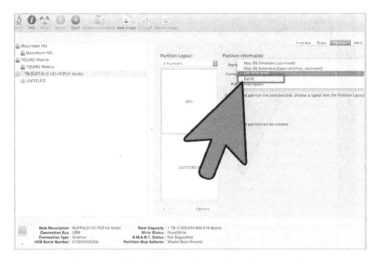

5. To format the disc using the chosen format, click "Erase"

6. Give your freshly formatted disc a try.

Configure the storage media as a backup disc.

1. Select System Settings from the Apple icon menu in the bottom left corner of your screen

2. In the sidebar, select General. subsequently, hit on Time Machine via the right

3. Either click the Add button (+) or select Add Backup Disc

4. Click Set Up Disc after selecting the linked storage device

5. As you set up:
   - To utilize the storage device for Time Machine, your Mac may ask if you wish to wipe it. Either remove it or choose an alternative backup volume or disc
   - Your Mac may inquire as to whether backups that were made on another

machine should be claimed by this one. If you want the backups to be included in this Mac's backups, you must claim them

- Once configured, your Mac starts using the storage device right away to create backups.

Making your device back up

1. Select Back Up Now from the Time Machine menu in the menu bar to make a backup right away. or hold off until the subsequent automated backup.
2. To halt, bypass, or monitor the progress of a backup, utilize the same menu. The date and time of the most recent backup, or the percentage of the current backup completed, are displayed at the top of the menu:

Backup is in progress   Backup is done

Utilize a backup to reinstate your Macbook

To move files from your Time Machine backup to your Mac, use Migration Assistant.

Use Migration Assistant

1. Re-install macOS if essential before moving on. For instance, you must first reinstall macOS if your Mac boots up with a flashing question mark. Check out how to download macOS again.
2. Verify that your Time Machine backup disc is powered on and attached to your Mac
3. Launch Mac Migration Assistant. It's located in your Applications folder's Utilities folder.
   - Proceed to the next step if your Mac launches with a setup assistant asking for information about your network and country. This is because the setup assistant comes with a migration assistant.
4. Choose the option to transfer from a Mac, Time (T) Machine backup, or begin loading the disc when prompted about how you wish to move your data. Next, select "Continue."

Migration Assistant

If you have information on another Mac or a Windows PC, you can transfer it to this Mac. You can also transfer information from a Time Machine backup or another startup disk.

How do you want to transfer your information?

○ From a Mac, Time Machine backup or Startup disk
　 From a Windows PC
　 To another Mac

Quit　　Continue

5. Click Proceed after selecting your Time Machine backup

6. Select a backup and press the Next button

7. Decide which data to send along

8. Get familiar with the meaning of transferring a user account before clicking Proceed. John Appleseed is an example user account in this illustration. Migration Assistant asks if you want to replace or rename an account if they are the same on your Mac:

   - Rename: The Time Machine backup account will show up on your Mac as an extra user, complete with a unique login and home folder

   - Replace: The Mac account with the same name will be replaced with the account from your Time Machine backup.

9. It may take hours to finish large transfers, and there may be periodic pauses. Perhaps you might begin in the evening and let the migration finish overnight. To begin the transfer, click Proceed.

207

10. To view the files from the migrated account on your Mac, log in to Migration Assistant when it has finished.

Book index

A

Accept a file or folder-sharing invitation, 50

Activate and Deactivate Stage Manager, 67

Activate Find My Mac., 188

Activate iCloud Pictures., 52

Activate Lost Mode, 192

Activate or deactivate the downtime schedule, 168

Activate the location services, 188

Activate two-factor verification on your Apple ID, 186

Add an album or folder, 136

Add or include widgets to your display desktop, 143

Adding and customizing widgets for Mac, 142

Adding Notification Centre widgets, 143

Additional features, 2

Adjust a sent text or SMS, 103

Adjust Mail's privacy settings on a Mac, 179

Adjust the linked display's resolution, 122

Adjust the music settings, 160

Adjust your system screen display language, 118

Allow individuals to work together in folders, 49

Always surf in privacy, 178

Answering or Taking a FaceTime group call, 175

Apple ID two-factor authentication, 186

Arrange tracks in Mac Music., 156

B

Backing up your Macbook, 199

Battery life history, 15

battery percentage, 13

Block or unblock senders on your mail, 180

Blocking senders, 180

Blocking text in messages on your Macbook, 106

Browse once secretly, 178

Browse secretly using Mac Safari., 177

C

Change the name or remove fingerprints, 65

Change the resolution of your Mac display, 122

Change the volume of the Music, 153

Charging your Macbook, 13

Check for songs via the iTunes, 147

Check if macOs Sonoma can work on your Mac, 5

Check out which device is Compatible with the new macOS 14, 5

Choose between a bright and dark theme for your Macbook, 138

Choosing your preferred language for every application, 118

Clear your browser history., 179

Collaborate & share folders using iCloud, 49

Color (hue) temperature, 141

Configure a child's screen time on a Mac, 163
Configure Find My on a Mac, 188
Configure the storage media as a backup disc., 203
Configure Touch ID, 63
Configure your Apple ID's data, 32
Connect to a secret WiFi network, 54
Control unwanted calls, 107
Convert audio file types in Mac Music, 159
Create a downtime schedule., 167
Create SharePlay to launch automatically, 152
Creating & controlling contacts in Mac Messages, 107
Creating a fresh contact, 107
Creating a pass key, 185
Creating or generating an Apple ID, 31
Crop a Mac Screenshot, 131
Custom Area Screenshot, 130
Customize your display, 109

D

Disable your AirTags or any item's Lost Mode in Find My on Mac, 193
Discover music in Mac Music via the filters, 149
Downloading & installing the new macOS Sonoma, 6
Dynamic or Lively Wallpapers, 136

E

Enhance Battery Charging, 14
Enlarge text and icons, 120

Enlarge text for certain applications, 120

F

Facetime on your Macbook Air, 172
Family and friends, 161
Family Sharing and iCloud configurations, 112
Find a device, 189
Find songs, 147
Find the Music files, 158
Find tracks in Music on Mac by using the column browser, 148
Formatting a New Drive, 201

H

High Power Mode, 14

I

iCloud, 47
Immediately turn downtime on or off., 169
Include a picture, 135
Include extra participants in a FaceTime video chat, 174
Increasing display size & icons, 119
Integrated Screenshot Cropping Tool, 131

J

Joining a FaceTime call on your Mac via a link, 176

K

Keep your Documents and Desktop folders on iCloud Drive, 48
Knowing simple Gestures, 28

L

Launch a fresh FaceTime group chat., 174
Locate a setting option in the System Settings, 114
Lock the screen, 110
Log in or out of your Apple ID on a Mac, 34
Log in to your Mac using Apple Sign, 182
Login with your Apple ID, 34
Low Power Mode, 14

M

Mac wallpaper settings, 135
Macbook Air Touch ID & trackpad, 61
Make a Wi-Fi connection., 56
Make use of Safari's privacy features., 177
Make your Memoji on Mac Messages, 106
Make your screen text & other icons bigger, 119
Making a video call via Facetime, 172
Making your device back up, 204
Managing and setting up Apple ID on a Mac, 30
Mark a gadget as lost on Mac., 191
Message someone on a Mac, 100

Modify a person's name to look differently in the sidebar, 108
modify Mac Stage Manager Settings, 76
Modify the Mac's Screenshot Save Location, 131
Modify the phone number displayed in the Lost Mode alert, 193
Modify the widget's settings., 144
Mouse gestures, 62
Moving or transferring files from one Macbook to a different one, 80
MUSIC, 147

N

Night Shift settings, 138

O

Open System Preference on your Macbook to locate options., 113
Organize and add songs to the queue, 155
Organize your Apple ID's media and buying preferences on a Mac, 34
Organize your files into a single Music folder., 159

P

Pair to an available WiFi network, 54
Pairing or Link your Macbook Air computer to the internet, 54
Pausing or muting a group FaceTime video call, 176

211

Personalize find MY, 194

personalize the desktop form, 27

Personalize the Mac's screen saver, 145

Personalize the menu bar and Control Centre., 112

Personalize the messages, 105

Personalize widgets, 144

Personalize your Mac's wallpaper, 134

Play music together on a Mac with SharePlay, 151

Play the Apple Music radio in Mac Music, 151

Playing a station, 151

Printing documents via your Macbook printer, 195

Privacy and security, 177

Put your music in order, 155

Q

Quit sharing a folder., 51

Quit using private browsing., 178

R

Reduce battery consumption., 16

Reject a FaceTime group video call, 176

Remember your forgotten passwords, 110

Restarting your device after installation or upgrade, 12

Restrict whoever has access to your Macbook camera, 181

S

Safeguard your data, 184

Schedule, 139

Screenshot via Complete Screen, 129

Screenshot via menu bar pop-up, 130

Search Apple songs, 147

Search for a gadget location, 190

See and control the files you've shared, 50

See the location of a gadget, 189

Select a paper size for your printed document on Mac, 196

Select a photo to utilize as your gadget's wallpaper., 136

Select a screen protector, 110

Select music from your preferred genres., 148

Send an email with a special, arbitrary address, 180

Sending an audio message via your Macbook, 105

Set Screen Time, 164

Set up a station, 151

Set up iCloud Keychain., 185

Set up macOS 14, 8

Set up your Apple ID mailing address and payment method, 33

Set up your Mac's Apple ID sign-in and security details, 33

Setting up the Night Shift, 139

Setup Apple Pay & Touch ID, 26

Setup iMessage, 100

Setup Messages, 100

Setup your Macbook Family Sharing, 161

Setup your new Macbook Air, 18

Sharing passphrase & passkeys with others, 111

Shuffle or replay tracks via your music, 154

Signing out or Exiting your Apple ID, 35

Sort using the pop-up menu, 157
Specifications, 2
Split Screen, 124
Stage Manager on Mac, 67
Stop or Close a FaceTime video
    chat, 173
Stop using iMessage, 100
Stop utilizing iCloud Pictures, 53
Storing folders in iCloud Drive on
    Mac, 48
Streaming suggested music from
    Apple Music, 150

T

Take the Notification Center's
    widgets down, 144
Taking a Screenshot, 129
Texting or sending text to groups,
    101
Toggle between AirTag and other
    items in Find My on Mac's Lost
    Mode, 192
Toggle on your device, 11
Toggle your Macbook off, 12
Trackpad gestures, 61
Troubleshooting, 198
Turn down a FaceTime video chat,
    173

U

Unblocking blocked senders., 180
Undoing a sent text or SMS, 103
Un-send or modify a message on
    Mac, 103
Update macOS., 112
Upgrading to the new macOS
    Sonoma, 5
Use a Mac in Split Screen Mode,
    127

Use Business Chat to send a text
    to a company, 102
Use Mac Music to listen to an
    online broadcast, 153
Use Mac's Stage Manager, 67
Use Mail on a Mac to Hide My
    Email, 180
Use Migration Assistant, 205
use of the Mac's trackpad and
    mouse motions, 61
Use Quick Look to view and edit
    files on a Mac., 57
Use Several Apps and Groups in
    Stage Manager, 73
Use USB to connect, 57
Use Your Screen Time, 177
Using find MY, 188
Using software updates, 9
Utilise a Single App with Stage
    Manager, 71
Utilize a Mac screen saver, 145
Utilize Autoplay, 155
Utilize Ethernet to pair your Mac
    to the web, 55
Utilize Mac iCloud Photos, 52
Utilize Mac Touch ID, 63
Utilize Mac widgets for iPhones,
    144
Utilize Mail Privacy Protection,
    179
Utilize Migration Assist, 81
Utilize Mission Control to split-
    screen, 126
Utilize Photos application to crop,
    133
Utilize Screen Time on Mac to
    schedule downtime, 166
Utilize Tapbacks in a text via your
    Macbook, 103
Utilize the Instant Hotspot, 56
Utilize the queue, 155

213

Utilize Touch ID to generate
procurement, 66
Utilize Touch ID to open your
Macbook, login, or swap users,
65
Utilize two-factor authentication
to log in and obtain a
verification code, 187
Utilize WiFi, 54
Utilize your Mac Split Screen, 124
Utilizing System Setups to
personalize your Macbook,
113

View and manage the storage on
your iCloud, 51
View item details on a Mac in Find
My, 194
View the battery-charged level, 15
View the music you've played
lately, 156
View your present location, 194

What is a Stage Manager?, 67
Widget, 142

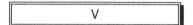

Verify the whereabouts of a
reported missing device, 191
Via Time Machine backup, 81

Your Mac's System Preferences,
109

Made in the USA
Las Vegas, NV
04 December 2024

13301866R00128